Reading & Writing Excellence

KEYS TO STANDARDS-BASED ASSESSMENT

Carol Alexander

STECK-VAUGHN
BERRENT
A Harcourt Company

www.steck-vaughn.com

ACKNOWLEDGMENTS

Project Author: Carol Alexander

Executive Editor: Carol Traynor

Senior Editor: Amy Losi

Editor II: Caren Churchbuilder

Editor I: Edward Nasello

Associate Editor: Christy Yaros

Project Consultant: Howard Berrent

Art Director: Frank Bruno

Design and Production: Susan Geer Associates, Inc.

Designer I: Julene Mays

Design Associate: Gregory Silverman

Cover Design: S. Michelle Wiggins

Photo Research: Sarah Fraser

Illustrators: Rose Mary Berlin

Elaine Garvin

Yuri Salzman

Lynn Titleman

Steck-Vaughn/Berrent is indebted to the following for permission to use material in this book:

page 9 "Turning Over A New Leaf." Text Copyright ©1987 by Johanna Hurwitz. Used by permission of HarperCollins Publishers.

page 18 "maggie and milly and molly and may." Copyright ©1956, 1984, 1991 by the Trustees for the E. E. Cummings Trust, from COMPLETE POEMS: 1904-1962 by E. E. Cummings, edited by George J. Firmage. Used by permission of Liveright Publishing Corporation.

page 31 "Anansi Tries to Steal All the Wisdom in the World" adapted by Matt Evans from Kids Zone - Myths and Tales. Courtesy of Afro-American Archives and Research Center, Baltimore, MD.

page 44 "Lightning Strikes." Reprinted by permission of SPIDER magazine, February 2000, Vol. 7, No. 2 ©2000 by Lisa Harkrader.

Photo Credits:

Cover photo: David Perry/©FPG International; p.24 ©Bob Daemmrich Photos, Inc.; p.25 ©Marc Romanelli/MCMXCVII/Image Bank; p.50 ©Superstock; p.51 ©Runa Schoenberger/Grant Heilman Photography; p.102 ©Bob Daemmrich Photo, Inc.; p.103©Jim Cummins/FPG International.

STECK-VAUGHN BERRENT

A Harcourt Company

www.steck-vaughn.com

ISBN 0-7398-3952-7

Copyright © 2002 Steck-Vaughn Company

Published by Steck-Vaughn/Berrent Publications, a division of Steck-Vaughn Company.

1 2 3 4 5 6 7 8 9 TPO 06 05 04 03 02

Table of Contents

Students are instructed to approach a selection and test question using the
Four *R*s: Ready, Read, Respond, Review.

Unit 1 introduces the three levels of comprehension—literal,
interpretive, and critical—and presents specific strategies designed
to assist students in answering multiple-choice and short-answer
questions. Each question is identified in the instruction by the type
of skill it covers.

Unit 2 explains how students can use graphic organizers to help them
answer essay questions. A graphic organizer accompanies each of four
selections. Students are given instruction in how to use the different
organizers to answer essay questions about the selections. Each
question is identified in the instruction by the type of skill it covers.

Unit 3 builds upon what was taught in the previous two units.
Students apply what they have learned to answer multiple-choice and
open-ended questions about various selections. There are hints to
help them answer each question. Each question is identified in the
hint by the type of skill it covers.

Unit 4 provides students with an opportunity to independently
practice the strategies they have learned. This unit may be used as
a test to assess students' learning and to simulate formal tests.

To the Teacher

Reading & Writing Excellence is a series of instructional books designed to prepare students to take standardized reading tests. It introduces the **Four *R*s,** a strategy that will enable students to read selections, understand what they have read, and answer multiple-choice and open-ended questions about the reading material. Special emphasis is given to using graphic organizers as prewriting aids for answering essay questions.

Many genres, such as fiction, nonfiction, poems, fables, and folk tales, are included. Some of the passages are taken from published, authentic literature, reflecting the type of instruction that exists in classrooms today. The questions accompanying each passage represent the different levels of comprehension.

The material in this book provides your students with step-by-step instruction that will maximize their reading success in classroom work as well as in testing situations.

The Four *R*s to Success

People follow plans every day. Plans show you how to put things together or what direction to take. Plans give you steps to follow when you are doing a task.

When you take a reading test, you need a plan that will help you understand a selection and answer questions about it. You can follow this plan by remembering the **Four *R*s: R**eady, **R**ead, **R**espond, **R**eview.

Ready Before you read, you need to get ready.

► **Set a purpose for reading**   Think about why you are reading. This will help you to focus. If you are reading to answer questions for a test, you will be looking for information. You will also be reading to understand how the different parts of the selection fit together.

► **Preview the selection**   When you preview, you look at something ahead of time. Try to find out as much about the selection as you can before you read it. Read the title and look at any pictures. Read any headings. You might even want to quickly read the first paragraph.

► **Make predictions**   Next, guess what the selection may be about. This is called making predictions.

Read The next step is to read the selection. You will better understand what you read if you take an active role.

► **Picture what you are reading**   For stories, ask yourself, "What will happen next?" Some selections give you information instead. For these, try to figure out what the next part of the selection will be about.

► **Ask questions**   As you read, ask yourself questions about things you might not understand. Take the time to guess what the answers might be. Then, reread parts of the selection to see if your answers are right.

➤ **Check your predictions**   Keep your predictions in mind as you read. Are things turning out the way you expected? Make new predictions as you get more information. Keep doing this until you have finished the selection.

Respond   Now you are ready to answer some questions about the selection.

➤ **Read the question**   Read each question carefully. If the question has choices, read those, too.

➤ **Think about it**   Think about which parts of the selection will help you figure out the answer. Reread those sections. For some questions, you will have to choose the answer. For other questions, you will be writing an answer. Before you write an answer, be sure to organize your thoughts.

➤ **Answer the question**   You are now ready to answer the question. For multiple-choice questions, more than one answer often sounds right. Be careful to choose the *best* answer. If you are writing your answer, be sure to include all the points you want to make.

Review   Take another look at your answer. For a multiple-choice question, make sure you picked the best choice. For an answer you wrote, make sure that you have answered all parts of the question. Does your answer make sense? Be sure to check your spelling, punctuation, and grammar.

• • •

Three Levels of Comprehension

In this unit you will learn how to answer questions at three "key" levels of comprehension.

LEVEL 1: *Find the Key* (Literal Level)

Look for information—At the literal level, you recall or recognize information. The information you need is stated right in the selection.

LEVEL 2: *Turn the Lock* (Interpretive Level)

Determine meaning—At the interpretive level, you use the information in the passage to figure out the answers to questions. You might be explaining meaning. Or, you might be using clues to draw conclusions. For this level, you must show that you understand the information in the selection. You must also know how the different parts fit together.

LEVEL 3: *Open the Door* (Critical Level)

Go beyond the text—At the critical level, you think about the selection and add what you know from your own experiences. You evaluate and extend meaning. You also make judgments about what you have read.

LEVEL I: Find the Key
Introduction to Literal Questions

A literal question will ask you to recall or recognize information. The answer to the question is found in the selection.

Types of literal questions may include the following:

► Identifying details from the selection
► Identifying the order of events
► Identifying cause-and-effect situations
► Identifying character traits

Identify key words

The key to answering a literal question is to find out where the answer is. Think about where this information might appear in the selection. Then identify key words in the question that might also appear in the passage. For example, look at the following question:

Who were the first native Americans?

To answer this question, you would look for the key words *native* and *Americans* in the selection. If you cannot find these words, look for words that mean about the same thing. Instead of *native*, you might look for *first peoples.* Or, you might look for words that tell about how people lived in groups, such as *tribes* or *clans.*

Find the clues

Sometimes you will not have key words to help you. Then you must think carefully about what the question is asking. Look at this question:

Which sentence tells the main idea of the passage?

Here there are no key words to look for, but the answer can still be found in the selection. First, you must know what a *main idea* is. It is the most important idea in the passage. So you would look for the one sentence that tells what the whole selection is about.

Answering Literal Questions

Now you will learn how to answer literal questions about a story.
Be sure to follow the **Four *R*s:**

4Rs

Ready—Get ready to read　　**R**espond—Answer the question

Read—Read the selection　　**R**eview—Check your answer

DIRECTIONS: Read this story about Lucas, a third-grader who likes to do things his own way. Then answer questions I through 8.

Turning Over a New Leaf

from *Class Clown*

by Johanna Hurwitz

"Here is a homework assignment for tomorrow," said Mrs. Hockaday.

Everyone groaned. The loudest protest came from Lucas. He hated homework. Lots of times he didn't even bother to do it. Instead he made up excuses about why his homework had not been done.

"It's a lovely autumn day outside," said their teacher. "So I want you each to bring one or two leaves that you find on the ground. Tomorrow we will identify them. There are many types of trees around here. It will be interesting to see what you find."

Cricket Kaufman raised her hand. "Don't you want us to write a report about our leaves as part of our homework?" she asked.

Lucas looked across the aisle at Cricket. He wished he had a spitball handy. What sort of stupid question was that?

Luckily, Mrs. Hockaday did not decide to have the third graders write reports. "Just leaves," she said, smiling. "But there is no excuse for anyone forgetting to bring them tomorrow. That means you, too, Lucas," she added. Lucas had become quite famous in class for not remembering to do his homework.

"I'll bring the most leaves of anyone," said Lucas. "See if I don't." He had suddenly remembered his promise to his mother. If he was going to turn over a new leaf, then he had to do his homework. The funny thing was that he was expected to bring an old leaf into class.

On the way home, Lucas noticed several of his classmates picking up leaves. He didn't bother. He had helped his father rake leaves in their backyard over the weekend. He knew there were several huge plastic bags full of leaves sitting in front of their house waiting for the garbage pickup the next day. Lucas thought he would just open one of the bags and take out a handful of leaves.

When he got home and looked at the bags, Lucas got an idea. Wouldn't it be funny if he brought a whole bag of leaves into his class tomorrow. He had told Mrs. Hockaday that he would bring more leaves than anyone else.

And it would certainly be worth the effort just to see the expression on Cricket Kaufman's face. Lucas tried to lift one of the bags but it was too heavy to carry all the way to school.

In the garage, Lucas had an old wagon that he used to play with when he was little. It would be perfect for hauling the bag of leaves to school the next day. He decided not to tell his parents about his plan. His mother would probably say that he didn't have to bring so many leaves to school. But she hadn't heard the tone that Mrs. Hockaday used when she said, "That means you, too, Lucas." Tomorrow he would show Mrs. Hockaday that he could do homework better than anyone else, if he wanted to.

DIRECTIONS: Read each question carefully. Darken the circle next to the correct answer choice or write your answer on the lines.

I What grade is Lucas in?

   Ⓐ Third grade

   Ⓑ Fourth grade

   Ⓒ Fifth grade

   Ⓓ Sixth grade

Find the Key

This question asks you to identify details from the story. Read the question and the choices carefully. The answer is found right in the selection. Look for a form of the key word *grade*. Once you have found the answer, you can make your choice.

2 After she raises her hand, Cricket Kaufman asks the teacher if the class should—

   Ⓕ put their leaves in a big garbage bag

   Ⓖ write a report about leaves

   Ⓗ draw pictures of leaves

   Ⓙ carry their leaves to school in a wagon

Find the Key

This is another question in which you must identify details. To find the answer to this question, reread the parts of the story where Cricket's name is first mentioned. What does she ask the teacher right after she raises her hand? Find the choice that best matches the question that Cricket asks the teacher.

3 What happens *first* in the story?

Ⓐ Lucas says he will bring in more leaves than anyone else in the class.

Ⓑ Cricket raises her hand and asks the teacher a question.

Ⓒ Lucas remembers there are bags full of leaves in front of his house.

Ⓓ Mrs. Hockaday asks her students to bring a leaf to school.

Find the Key

This question asks you to identify the order of events. You probably have a good idea which event happened first just from reading the story. Go back and find each event in the story. Then put the events in order. Which was the first to happen?

4 Mrs. Hockaday reminds Lucas to do his homework because—

Ⓕ he is not going to school the next day

Ⓖ he is not paying attention

Ⓗ he often forgets to do his homework

Ⓙ he wants Cricket to do his homework for him

Find the Key

In this question, you must identify a cause-and-effect situation. Why does Mrs. Hockaday remind Lucas to do his homework? To find the right answer, reread the part of the story where Mrs. Hockaday tells students to remember to bring in their leaves. What does the teacher think of as she repeats the instructions? Why does she mention Lucas's name in particular?

5 Lucas does not bother to look for a leaf on the ground because—

    Ⓐ he decides not to do his homework after all

    Ⓑ he wants to climb a tree to find a nice leaf

    Ⓒ he knows there are bags full of leaves at his house

    Ⓓ he decides to borrow a leaf from a friend

Find the Key

Here you must identify details from the story. The answer is in the story. To find the right answer, reread the part of the story where Lucas is walking home from school. What is he thinking about? How does he plan to get a leaf?

6 Why does Lucas groan loudly when his teacher says she is going to give a homework assignment?

    Ⓕ He does not like to look for leaves.

    Ⓖ He wants to play baseball after school.

    Ⓗ He does not like homework.

    Ⓙ He is too tired to do any more work.

Find the Key

This question asks you to identify a character trait, or something about Lucas. Reread the beginning of the story. The answer is right there. Read how Lucas protested the loudest. Then read the sentence that comes next. This is where you will find your answer.

7 Why does Lucas decide to keep his plan a secret from his parents?

_____

_____

_____

_____

_____

_____

Find the Key

For this question, you do not have choices to pick from. You will have to write your answer in a sentence or two. Here you must identify details again. You will find the correct answer in the story. Reread the ending. Look for the key word *parents* to find the answer.

8 Why does Lucas want to bring in a whole bag of leaves tomorrow, instead of just a few leaves?

_____

_____

_____

_____

_____

_____

Find the Key

Once again, you must identify details. Remember, this is a literal question. You'll find the answer somewhere in the story. Go back to where the bag of leaves is first mentioned. This is near the end of the story. Read the last two paragraphs of the story again.

LEVEL 2: Turn the Lock
Introduction to
Interpretive Questions

A detective looks at different pieces of information to find answers. When you answer an interpretive question, you put together different pieces of a selection to determine its meaning.

Types of interpretive questions may include the following:

► Interpreting character traits
► Interpreting vocabulary
► Determining the main idea
► Summarizing information
► Drawing conclusions

Unlock the answer

To answer an interpretive question, you must become a detective. Before a detective can look for clues, he or she must know what to look for. You can tell what to look for by examining the question.

Suppose you had to answer a question about *Beauty and the Beast,* a story in which a beautiful young woman falls in love with a beast. Look at the following question:

Why does the young woman fall in love with the beast?

The answer will not be right there in the story for you to find. You have to think carefully about what you have read to figure it out. You would need to reread the parts where the young woman and the beast talk to each other. How does the beast act toward the young woman?

Put the clues together

After you have reread parts of the selection, think about what you have read. Then, like a detective, put the clues together to draw a conclusion.

In the question above, you might find that the beast was kind and gentle with the young woman. Perhaps they shared things in common. These clues show you that the woman could overlook the beast's appearance and fall in love with his inner self.

Answering Interpretive Questions

Now you will learn how to answer interpretive questions about a poem.
Remember to follow the **Four *R*s:**

4Rs

Ready—Get ready to read

Read—Read the selection

Respond—Answer the question

Review—Check your answer

DIRECTIONS: **Read this poem about four girls who spend a day at the beach. Then answer questions 1 through 6.**

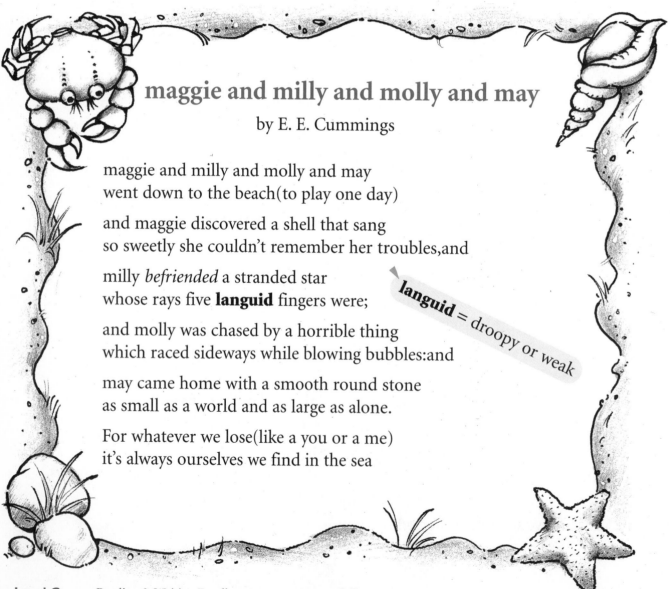

maggie and milly and molly and may
by E. E. Cummings

maggie and milly and molly and may
went down to the beach(to play one day)

and maggie discovered a shell that sang
so sweetly she couldn't remember her troubles,and

milly *befriended* a stranded star
whose rays five **languid** fingers were;

and molly was chased by a horrible thing
which raced sideways while blowing bubbles:and

may came home with a smooth round stone
as small as a world and as large as alone.

For whatever we lose(like a you or a me)
it's always ourselves we find in the sea

languid = droopy or weak

DIRECTIONS: Read each question carefully. Darken the circle next to the correct answer choice or write your answer on the lines.

I What do the girls do at the beach?

Ⓐ They blow bubbles.

Ⓑ They play in the water.

Ⓒ They look for new things.

Ⓓ They play a special game.

Turn the Lock

This question asks you to give a summary of what the girls do at the beach. Reread the poem. What does each girl do? Now look at the answer choices. Do the girls blow bubbles? Do they play in the water? Do they look for new things? Or do they play a special game?

2 In this poem, the word *befriended* means—

Ⓕ found

Ⓖ got to know

Ⓗ picked up

Ⓙ named

Turn the Lock

This is a vocabulary question. The word *befriended* may be new to you. Have you ever heard it used before? Reread the part of the poem that has the word. Does this give you any clues to the word's meaning? Look at the word itself. Does the word give you any clues to its meaning?

3 This poem is *mostly* about—

Ⓐ four friends playing by the sea

Ⓑ a girl who finds a special seashell

Ⓒ four friends who get lost by the sea

Ⓓ a girl who is chased by a thing on the beach

Turn the Lock

The main idea of a poem is what it is mostly about. The main idea usually is not stated in the poem. You need to read the poem and add up clues to figure it out. To find the main idea of this poem, think about the different things that happen to the girls. Where do they happen? How are these things the same?

4 You can tell from the poem that—

Ⓕ people like to sing when they are by the sea

Ⓖ molly found a fish by the sea

Ⓗ the sea is a special place

Ⓙ molly probably does not like the sea

Turn the Lock

The question asks you to conclude something from the poem. Read the answer choices. Then reread the poem. Does the poem lead you to believe that most people like to sing when they are by the sea? Do you know for sure that the "horrible thing" Molly found was a fish? Does the poem lead you to believe that most people enjoy spending time by the sea? Do you know that Molly dislikes the sea?

5 Read these lines from the poem.

> **and maggie discovered a shell that sang**
> **so sweetly she couldn't remember her troubles...**

How do you think a shell can sing?

_____

_____

_____

_____

_____

_____

Turn the Lock

Here you must interpret words. Find these lines in the poem. Reread the lines. Think about how a seashell can sing. What do you hear when you put a certain type of shell up to your ear? Think of a way to describe this sound. Write your answer on the lines.

6 How was Molly's day at the beach different from May's?

_____

_____

_____

_____

_____

_____

_____

Turn the Lock

Now you must compare the two girls in the poem. Reread the parts of the poem that talk about Molly and May. What happens to Molly? How do you think she felt? What happens to May? How do you think she felt? How is Molly's experience different from May's?

LEVEL 3: Open the Door
Introduction to Critical Questions

For a critical question, you must go beyond the words on the page. You bring in your own experiences to evaluate and extend meaning. You also make judgments about what you have read.

Types of critical questions may include the following:

▶ Analyzing the situation
▶ Predicting outcomes
▶ Determining the author's purpose
▶ Extending the passage
▶ Evaluating the passage

Step through the door

Now, you are going to become a judge. You will still look for clues to answer a question. But you will also study the information, decide how important it is, and make judgments about it.

Let's think about the story "Turning Over a New Leaf." Recall the characters Lucas and Cricket. Here is a critical question about these characters.

Do you think two people who dislike each other can ever become good friends?

You cannot find the answer in the story. This question is asking for your opinion. You must make a judgment based on the story and on your own experiences.

Make a case

Sometimes, we have to study a question to come up with a good answer. Think about your own friends. Did you like each person right away?

Next think about the story. It is realistic. The author could be describing students in your class. What is a true friendship based on?

Form your opinion to answer the question.

Answering Critical Questions

Now you will learn how to answer critical questions about two passages.
Don't forget to follow the **Four R s**:

Ready—Get ready to read   **R**espond—Answer the question
Read—Read the selection   **R**eview—Check your answer

**DIRECTIONS: Read this passage about ways to save water in our daily
lives. Think about why it is important to save fresh water. Then answer
questions 1 and 2.**

Let's Help Save Water

People need fresh water to drink and bathe. Did you know that only
about three percent of the water on Earth is fresh? Most of this fresh water
comes from arctic icecaps and glaciers.

People use a lot of fresh water. Most
people use about 100 gallons of fresh water
every day! People need fresh water, but they
sometimes waste it. This is dangerous. We
should save water, or we may run out of
it someday.

There are many things that you can do to
help save water. Turn off the water faucet
when you brush your teeth. Fill up your
bathtub only halfway instead of filling it to
the top. Do you wash dishes? Washing dishes
wastes a lot of water. Try filling up a basin
with soapy water. Then fill another basin
with clean water. Wash the dishes in the
soapy water. Then rinse them in the clean

water. This way, you do not have to leave the water running while you wash dishes.

When you are waiting for the water in your sink or bath to get hot, don't waste the cold water. Fill up a jug with this cold water. Use the cold water to water plants or rinse dishes.

Did you know that each time you flush the toilet, you use about four gallons of water? Only flush the toilet when you need to flush it. Don't use the toilet as a trash can.

Your parents can help save water, too. They can purchase low-flush toilets that use less water. They can also buy special showerheads that use less water. They can even buy washing machines and dishwashers that save water.

Do your parents own a car? If they do, you can save water when you wash the car. Turn off the hose when you are putting soap on the car. Only run the water when you rinse the car.

Do you have a garden? If you do, water your garden early in the morning or late in the afternoon. Don't water your garden in the middle of the day. The bright midday sun dries up the water too fast. And don't water plants and flowers if it is supposed to rain.

Think about how your family uses water. There may be some ways that water is wasted in your home. Make a list of these ways. Then think of how you can save water. By saving water, you will help make sure we have lots of fresh water in the future.

DIRECTIONS: Read each question carefully. Then write your answer on the lines.

1   Why do you think it is important to save fresh water?

_____

_____

_____

_____

_____

_____

Open the Door

This question asks about the meaning of the passage. Reread the beginning of the passage. How much of the earth's water is fresh? Why do you think it is important to save it? Make a list of reasons. At least one reason should come from the article. Other reasons may be your own. Think about what would happen if we didn't have fresh water. Write your answer above.

2 Think about how your family uses water. What can you do to help save water around your home?

_____

_____

_____

_____

_____

_____

Open the Door

Here you must extend the passage and think about how it fits into your life. List a few ways your family uses water. Then go back to the passage and reread some ways to save water. Which of these ways could you use around your own home? You might also think of a few new ways to save water on your own.

Speak Out

You have read how people can save water. Think about how you or someone in your family uses water wisely. Prepare a short speech about how this is done. Then give your speech to the class.

Summary

In this unit, you have learned how to answer questions at three "key" levels of comprehension.

Find the Key	*Turn the Lock*	*Open the Door*

"Literal"	**"Interpretive"**	**"Critical"**
Look for information	*Determine meaning*	*Go beyond the text*

Remember that no matter what type of question you answer, you should always use the **Four *R*s:** **R**eady, **R**ead, **R**espond, **R**eview.

Ready—**Get ready to read**

- ► Set a purpose for reading
- ► Preview the selection
- ► Make predictions

Read—**Read the selection**

- ► Picture what you are reading
- ► Ask questions
- ► Check your predictions

Respond—**Answer the question**

- ► Read the question
- ► Think about it
- ► Answer the question

Review—**Check your answer**

Graphic Organizers: The Key to Answering Essay Questions

The Essay Question

In Unit 1 you answered both multiple-choice and short-answer questions. Another type of test question is an essay question. For an essay question, you must write one or two paragraphs. Essay questions often make you think more than other types of questions. You must recall and understand details of the passage you just read.

Get Organized!

You know how hard it is to find something in a messy drawer. You look and look, but the thing you are looking for escapes you in the clutter. But finding something in a well-organized drawer is very easy. In the same way, you can answer an essay question more easily if you are organized before you begin to write.

A **graphic organizer** is a picture that lets you put your ideas in order. A graphic organizer helps you gather the information you need to answer your essay question. Once you organize your thoughts and ideas, it will be easier for you to write your essay.

In this unit, you will learn how to use different kinds of graphic organizers to answer essay questions. But first, look at the next page. Here are some things to think about before and after you begin to write.

Before You Write

Before you write anything, ask yourself some questions:

1. *What is my topic?* What will you be writing about? State the topic in a few words. This will help you focus your writing.

2. *Why am I writing?* Think about the purpose of the essay. Usually you write to explain something, persuade someone, entertain someone, or describe something.

3. *Who will read my writing?* This is your audience. Your teacher will probably be your audience for a test.

 # After You Write

After you write your essay, use this list to check your writing.

Revise:

❑ Did you answer the question asked?

❑ Does your essay have a beginning and an ending?

❑ Is each idea in a separate paragraph?

❑ Does each paragraph have a main idea?

❑ Does each paragraph have details to support the main idea?

❑ Do all of your sentences make sense?

Edit:

❑ Are all of your words spelled correctly?

❑ Did you use correct punctuation in each sentence?

❑ Did you use a capital letter at the beginning of each sentence?

DIRECTIONS: Read the following story about Anansi, a popular character in African folktales. Then you will use a Main Idea Map. It will help you explain why Anansi is not wise.

Anansi Tries to Steal All the Wisdom in the World

adapted by Matt Evans

Anansi the spider knew that he was not wise. He was very clever, and could **outwit** many different people, but he knew that he did not have very much wisdom.

This bothered him a great deal, but he did not know what to do about it.

Then one day he had a clever thought. "I know," he said to no one in particular, "if I can get all of the wisdom in the village and put it in a **hollow gourd,** I will be very wise indeed. In fact, I would be the wisest of all!"

So he set out to find a suitable gourd and then began his journey to collect the village's wisdom.

He went from door to door, asking everyone to give some of their wisdom. The people chuckled at poor Anansi, for they knew that of all the creatures, it was he that needed some wisdom the most. So each put a bit in his gourd and wished him well on his search.

Soon Anansi's gourd was overflowing with wisdom and he could hold no more. He now needed to find a place to store it.

"I am certainly the wisest person in the world now, but if I don't find a good hiding place for my wisdom I may surely lose it."

outwit = trick or be smarter than
hollow gourd = large piece of fruit or vegetable that is empty on the inside

He looked around and spotted a tall, tall tree.

"Ah," he said to himself, "if I could hide my wisdom high in that tree, I would never have to worry about someone stealing it from me!"

So Anansi set out to climb the **towering** tree.

He first took a cloth band and tied it around his waist. Then he tied the heavy gourd to the front of his belly where it would be safe.

As he began to climb, however, the gourd full of wisdom kept getting in the way. He tried and tried, but he could not **make progress around it.**

Soon Anansi's youngest son walked by.

"What are you doing Father?" asked the little spider.

"I am climbing this tree with my gourd full of wisdom," Anansi replied.

"But Father," said the son, "wouldn't it be much easier if you tied the gourd behind you instead of in front?"

Anansi sat quietly for a very long time before saying, "Shouldn't you be going home now?"

The son skipped down the path and when he had disappeared, Anansi moved the gourd so that it was behind him and **proceeded** up the tree with no problems at all.

When he had reached the top, he cried out, "I walked all over and collected so much wisdom that I am the wisest person ever, but still my baby son is wiser than me. Take back your wisdom!"

He lifted the gourd high over his head and spilled **its contents** into the wind. The wisdom blew far and wide and settled across the land.

And this is how wisdom came into the world.

towering = very tall
make progress around it = make his way around it
proceeded = made his way
its contents = what was inside the gourd

Main Idea Map

The main idea is the most important idea in a passage. It is what the passage is all about. There are times when you will have an essay question that asks you what the story is about, or what the main idea of the story is. Using a **Main Idea Map** will help you organize your thoughts so that you can answer this type of essay question better. Look at the **Main Idea Map** below.

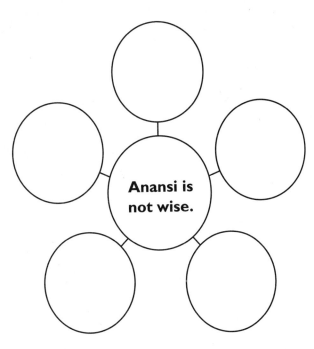

A **Main Idea Map** is made up of bubbles. There is one large bubble in the middle. This is where you write the main idea of the passage you just read. You can see that this bubble is already filled in on the **Main Idea Map** above. A main idea of the story you just read is that Anansi is not wise.

Attached to the large bubble are smaller bubbles. In these smaller bubbles you are to write details from the story that help to prove the main idea you wrote in the large bubble. You can add as many bubbles as you need. The number of bubbles depends on how many details from the story that help prove your main idea. There are some details in the story you just read that help prove Anansi is not wise.

Now let's try to fill in the same **Main Idea Map** on the next page.

Let's fill in this **Main Idea Map** to help answer a question about the story you just read. Read the essay question and instructions on page 35.

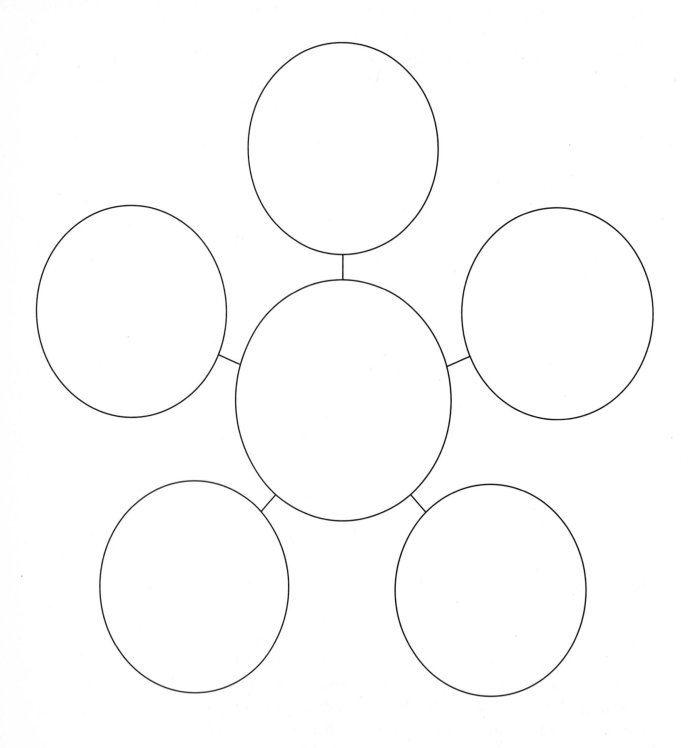

Essay Question: In the story you just read, Anansi shows that he is not wise. Explain how Anansi is not wise. Use details and examples from the story.

1. The essay question gives you the main idea. It says that, "In the story you just read, Anansi shows that he is not wise." Write this as the main idea in the large bubble of the **Main Idea Map.** Write **Anansi is not wise.**

2. Next, you have to find the details in the story that help prove the main idea. What does Anansi do in the story that shows he is not wise? Ask yourself these questions: Can someone really steal all the wisdom in the world? What does Anansi's son say to him in the story? Write each detail from the story in a bubble attached to the large bubble in the middle.

Now that you have filled in the **Main Idea Map,** use it to answer the essay question at the top of the page. Write your answer on a separate sheet of paper.

Turn the Lock

This question asks you to draw a conclusion based on details in the story. It is an interpretive question. You must put together different pieces of the passage to determine its meaning.

Start your essay by stating the main idea that you wrote in your **Main Idea Map.** Then give the details from the map that help prove the main idea. Make sure you write in your paragraph that these details explain how Anansi is not wise.

Remember to **Review.** When you are done, make sure that your writing is the best it can be by using the checklist on page 30.

DIRECTIONS: Read this poster about summer classes at the Green Mountain Art School. Then you will use a Venn Diagram. It will help you write about the two different groups of classes offered.

Summer Classes

Looking for something fun to do this summer? Take some classes at the Green Mountain Art School. Beginners are welcome!

ARTS AND CRAFTS

Make Your Own Jewelry

Do you want to make your own jewelry? Learn how to make beautiful bracelets and necklaces. Both boys and girls are welcome. Students will display their jewelry in a show at the end of the summer.

Paint with Oils

Learn how to paint like a real artist. Paint pictures of people and outdoor scenes. Everyone will enter their paintings in a contest at the end of the summer.

DRAMA AND DANCE

Mini Musical

Learn what it is like to be a star in a real musical! Students sing and dance and put on a wonderful show.

Tap Dancing

Learn how to tap dance to modern music. Students put on a show at the end of the summer. Tap shoes are required.

Venn Diagram

An essay question might ask you to compare and contrast two things. When you compare and contrast, you tell how two things are alike and how they are different. You might be asked to compare and contrast two people, things, or places that you have just read about.

Using a **Venn Diagram** will help you compare two things to find out what is alike about them. It will also help you contrast two things to find out what is different about them. Look at the **Venn Diagram** below.

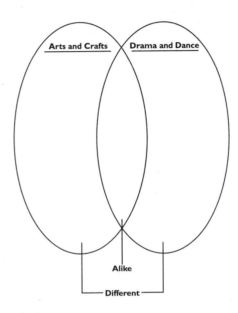

A **Venn Diagram** is made up of two large ovals, or circles, that overlap each other. Each oval represents one thing. The name of each thing being compared and contrasted goes at the top of the oval. The two things being compared and contrasted here are "Arts and Crafts" and "Drama and Dance" from the poster you just read. Each group of classes has some things that are like the other group. Each group also has some things that are different from the other group.

Think about how the "Arts and Crafts" classes are different from the "Drama and Dance" classes. These differences go in the *outside parts* of the ovals. Think about how the "Arts and Crafts" classes are like the "Drama and Dance" classes. This information goes in the *middle part* of the oval.

Now let's try to fill in the same **Venn Diagram** on the next page.

Let's fill in this **Venn Diagram** to help answer a question about the poster you just read. Read the essay question and instructions on page 39.

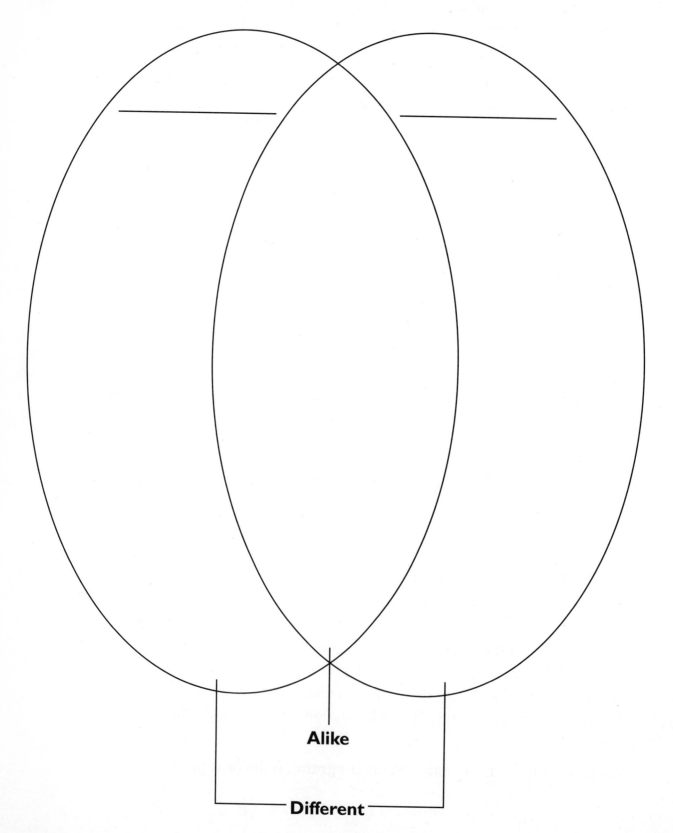

Alike

Different

Essay question: How are the "Arts and Crafts" classes different from the "Drama and Dance" classes? How are they the same? Use details from the poster to explain your answer.

1. To answer this question, you must compare and contrast the "Arts and Crafts" classes with the "Dance and Drama" classes. On the line at the top of the first oval, write **Arts and Crafts.** On the top line of the second oval, write **Drama and Dance.**

2. Next, reread the classes on the poster. Look for clues to tell you what is different about the two groups. Do you learn different things in each of the groups? Write the differences in the *outside parts* of the correct ovals. Things that are different about "Arts and Crafts" classes go in the first oval. Things that are different about "Drama and Dance" classes go in the second oval.

3. Now think about how both groups of classes are the same. Is some kind of show given at the end of each class? Can beginners take these classes? Write how the groups are the same in the *middle part* of the ovals.

Now that you have filled in the **Venn Diagram,** use it to answer the essay question at the top of the page. Write your answer on a separate sheet of paper.

Turn the Lock

Here you must compare and contrast two different classes. This is an interpretive question. You must put together different pieces of the passage to determine its meaning.

Look at the graphic organizer. Use what you listed to write your essay. First write how the two groups are different. Then write how they are the same. Make sure to clearly state the details that you listed in the **Venn Diagram.**

Remember to **Review.** Check your writing on page 30.

DIRECTIONS: Read the following story about a boring afternoon that suddenly becomes exciting. Then you will use a Sequence Map. It will help you write about what you think will happen next.

Jared's Boring Afternoon

Jared Parker trudged down Main Street behind his mother. She was going to the beauty shop for a haircut. Jared had to go, too. His mother said he was not old enough to stay home alone. He kicked a pebble along the sidewalk. What a boring afternoon! He wished he were at the park kicking a soccer ball with his friends.

"I hope you will be patient this time," his mother said. "Maybe we could stop for ice cream afterwards, okay?"

"Can I at least wait outside while you get your hair cut?" Jared asked.

"Well, all right," replied his mother. "Just as long as you stay by the window where I can see you."

Jared's mother entered the beauty shop and found a chair by the window. Jared leaned against the outside wall of the building. The sun felt too hot. He wanted to go home. Just then a spotted dog wandered up to him, wagging its tail. It sniffed Jared's hands. Jared reached into his pocket and pulled out a pack of crackers. He fed the crackers to the dog and patted its head.

Jared didn't know much about dogs, but he knew this dog was a Dalmatian. They had a dog just like this at the fire station nearby. Jared shook the dog's paw and then peered into the window to see his mother.

Suddenly, a loud noise arose from down the street. It was the fire alarm! The Dalmatian spun around and sprinted down Main Street toward Elm Street. So this is the firehouse dog, thought Jared excitedly. He took off after the dog, but then stopped short. His mother would be furious if he disappeared—but he just had to see where the fire was!

Sequence Map

The word *sequence* means the order in which events happen. Sometimes an essay question will ask you about the sequence of events in a story. The question may ask you to retell the story in your own words or to predict what will happen next in the story. A **Sequence Map** will help you organize the events of the story so that you can answer this type of essay question better. Look at the **Sequence Map** below.

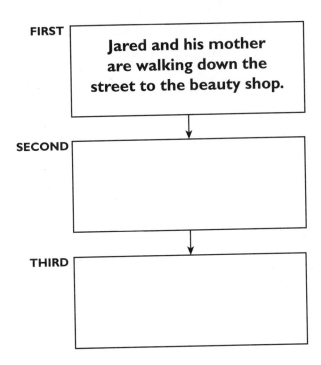

FIRST

Jared and his mother are walking down the street to the beauty shop.

SECOND

THIRD

A **Sequence Map** is made up of boxes that run in a line down the page. The boxes are joined by arrows pointing downward. In the boxes you write the events that happened in the story. The first event of the story goes in the box at the top, which is labeled "First." The first event of the story you just read is that Jared Parker walks down the street with his mother to get her hair cut.

The second event of the story goes in the second box of the **Sequence Map,** and the third event goes in the third box. You can use as many boxes as you need, until you list all of the events of the story. The box at the bottom of the **Sequence Map** should have the very last event of the story.

Now let's try to fill in the same **Sequence Map** on the next page.

Let's fill in the **Sequence Map** below to help you answer a question about the story you just read. Read the essay question and instructions on page 43.

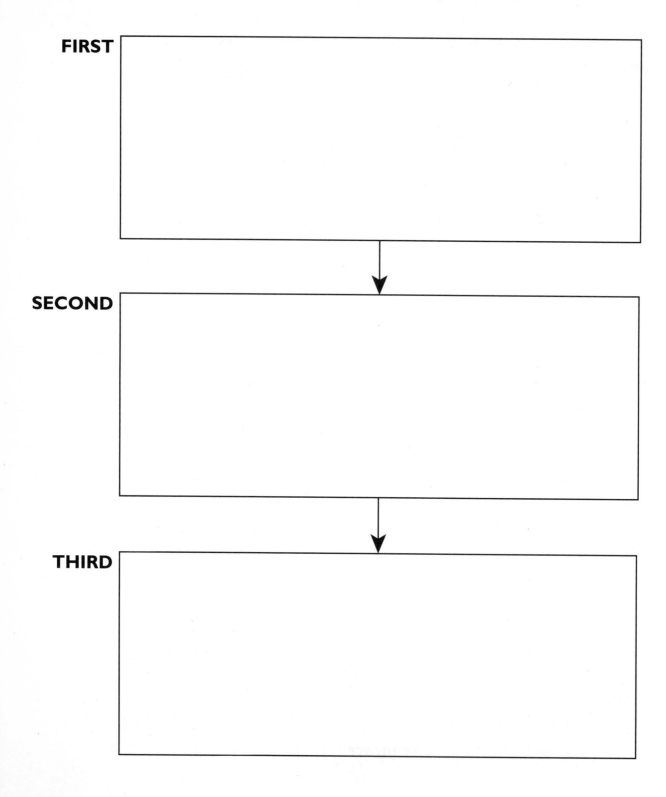

FIRST

SECOND

THIRD

Essay Question: What do you think will happen next in the story? Use the events from the story to write what Jared will decide to do.

1. The question asks you to predict what will happen next in the story. To do this, you must first organize the events that have already happened. Look back at the story. What did Jared have to do with his mother? Write this event in the first box.

2. Then look back to find out what event happened next in the story. What happened when Jared stayed outside waiting for his mother? This is the second event. Write it in the second box.

3. Last, what happened when Jared and the dog heard the fire alarm? Write the event in the third box. This is the last box in the organizer.

Now that you have filled in the **Sequence Map,** use it to answer the essay question at the top of the page. Write your answer on a separate sheet of paper.

Open the Door

This question asks you to extend the story and predict what will happen next. This is a critical question. You must go beyond the text and make a judgment about what you have read.

Look at what you wrote in the **Sequence Map.** You will use these events in the story to predict what Jared might do after the dog runs off toward the fire station. Make sure your prediction is based on the events in the map.

Remember the fourth **R**. After you finish, use the checklist on page 30 to review your writing.

DIRECTIONS: Read the following poem about an evening when the lights go out. Then you will use a Setting Map. It will help you explain what it is like for the speaker in the poem when the lights go out.

Lightning Strikes

by Lisa Harkrader

The TV set crackled.
The VCR stopped.
The microwave quit with my popcorn half popped.
My hard drive shut down with a hiss and a spark.
The lights flickered once,
then the whole house went dark.

I let out a sigh, found a flashlight, and stumbled
my way through the house in the blackness. I mumbled,
"This Saturday night sure is turning out rotten."
Then my light flashed on something I'd almost forgotten.
I tiptoed up to it and took a good look.
I smiled, and curled up with my light…
and a book.

Setting Map

The *setting* of a passage is where and when events happen. A setting is often described by what you can see, hear, smell, touch, and taste. You can use all of these descriptions to show the setting of a passage you just read. A **Setting Map** helps you to organize some of these details so that you can answer an essay question about the setting of a passage. Look at the **Setting Map** below.

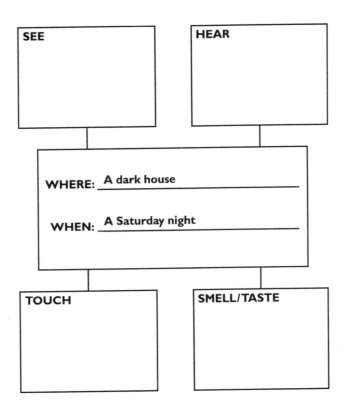

A **Setting Map** is made up of boxes. There is a box in the middle. This is for you to write where and when the story takes place. The poem you just read takes place in a dark house on a Saturday night.

Attached to the middle box are more boxes. Each of these boxes is labeled with a different sense—see, hear, touch, and smell/taste. Use the boxes to fill in details about things that are seen, heard, touched, smelled, or tasted in the passage. Write as many details from the poem as you can find. These details help describe the setting of the poem.

Now let's try to fill in the same **Setting Map** on the next page.

Let's fill in the **Setting Map** below to help answer a question about the poem you just read. Read the essay question and instructions on page 47.

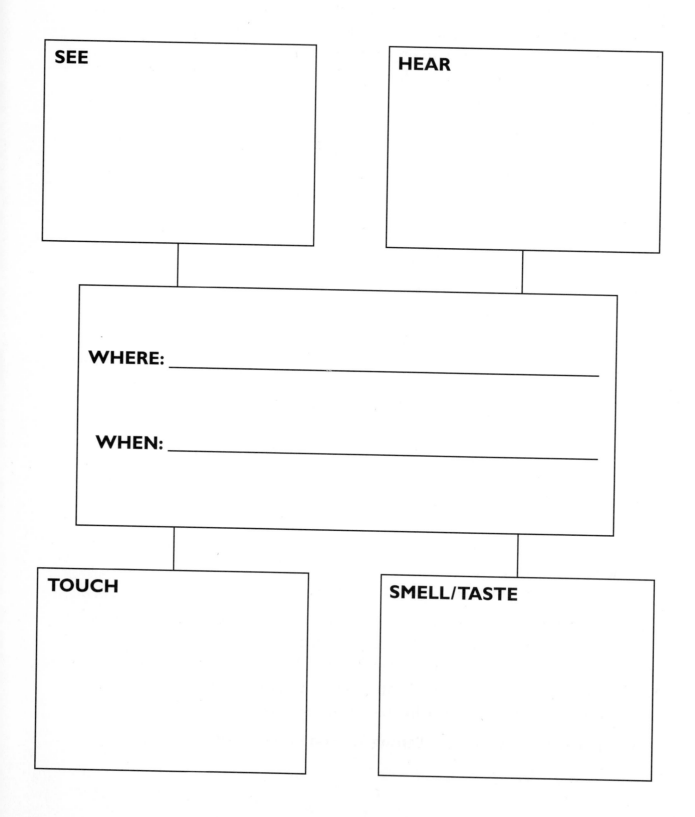

SEE

HEAR

WHERE: _____

WHEN: _____

TOUCH

SMELL/TASTE

Essay question: Explain what it is like for the narrator when the lights go out. Use examples from the poem.

1. First, fill in the middle box. Where and when does the poem take place?

2. Next, fill in the first box labeled "SEE." What does the narrator see in the poem? Write these details in the box marked "SEE".

3. Next, fill in the second box labeled "HEAR." What does the narrator hear in the poem? Write these details in the box marked "HEAR."

4. Then, fill in the third box labeled "TOUCH." Reread the poem to find out what the narrator touched as she stumbled around the dark house. Then write these details in the box marked "TOUCH."

5. Finally, fill in the fourth box labeled "SMELL/TASTE." Look again at the first part of the poem. Can you find a detail that suggests what the narrator might have smelled? Write this detail in the box marked "SMELL/TASTE."

Now that you have filled in the **Setting Map,** use it to answer the essay question at the top of the page. Write your answer on a separate sheet of paper.

Turn the Lock

Here you must summarize the poem by describing the setting. This is an interpretive question. You must put together different pieces of the poem to determine its meaning.

Start your essay by stating where and when the poem takes place. This is in the middle box of the **Setting Map.** Then give the details from the map that help describe the setting of the story. Make sure you draw some conclusions about how the narrator felt about her experiences that night.

Don't forget the fourth **R** in the **Four Rs:** **R**eady, **R**ead, **R**espond, **R**eview. Make sure that your writing is the best it can be. To do this, use the checklist on page 30.

Summary

You can use graphic organizers to help you recall and understand what you have read. Graphic organizers can also help you answer essay questions about a passage. They help you put your ideas and thoughts in order before you begin to write.

You have learned about the following graphic organizers:

Main Idea Map

Venn Diagram

Sequence Map

Setting Map

 Remember that when answering an essay question, you should always use the **Four Rs:** Ready, Read, Respond, Review. When you review your work, use a checklist such as the one on page 30.

Guided Practice

Now you are going to practice what you have learned by reading several selections. You will be asked to answer multiple-choice, short-answer, and essay questions about what you have read. These questions will be at the three key levels of comprehension: literal, interpretive, and critical. You will be given a hint to help you answer each question.

Whatever type of selection you read or question you answer, you should always follow the **Four *R*s:**

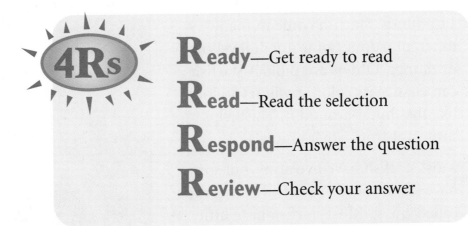

4Rs

Ready—Get ready to read

Read—Read the selection

Respond—Answer the question

Review—Check your answer

DIRECTIONS: Read this passage about an unusual sea animal. Then answer questions 1 through 7. Darken the circle next to the correct answer choice or write your answer on the lines.

Stars of the Sea

1   Have you ever seen a starfish? Starfish are amazing animals. They live in the sea, so they are sometimes called sea stars. There are many different kinds of starfish. Some are very tiny. Others can grow to be over two feet wide! The largest starfish ever found weighed over 11 pounds. Starfish come in many different colors. Some are dull yellow or orange. Others are pink. A starfish can change its color. It will try to look like the things around it. This helps protect it from other animals.

2   Most starfish have five arms, but some have six or more. A starfish's arms are called "rays." Most starfish have little spines all over their bodies. However, some starfish are very soft. The sunflower starfish is a soft starfish. A starfish does not have a brain, but it can touch, smell, and taste things. It does not have eyes, but it can sense light.

3   Starfish live in water all over the world. Most live in shallow water, but some live in deep water. Starfish can live in many places because they will eat almost anything. For example, a bat starfish likes to eat a kind of seaweed called kelp. But a bat starfish will eat other plants, or even small animals, too.

4   A starfish crawls as slow as a snail. When it moves, its mouth faces downward. Its pointed rays stick out from the center of its body. It can move its rays in many different ways. This helps it fit into small spaces between rocks. Each ray has rows of sticky feet on the bottom. These feet look like small tubes. A starfish sticks its feet to rocks and plants. It uses its feet to move and eat. Have you ever tried to pull a starfish off of a rock? It is a very hard thing to do. This *ability* helps protect the starfish from enemies.

5   A starfish eats in a very strange way. It eats smaller animals whole. If it wants to eat a clam or a mussel, the starfish opens the shell with its rays. Then it slips its stomach between the two halves of the shell. If it wants to eat a larger animal, it can stick its stomach outside of its body! A starfish will pull its stomach back into its body once it has finished eating.

A starfish is shown eating a mussel.

6   Starfish have other amazing abilities. A starfish lays eggs like many other animals, but it can also create new starfish from its own body parts. A young starfish may grow out of another starfish's arm. If another animal catches a starfish, it can "let go" of an arm and swim away! A new arm will grow to replace the old one.

1 A starfish can live in many different places because—

Ⓐ it moves very quickly

Ⓑ it can live on land or in water

Ⓒ it eats many types of food

Ⓓ it can grow new rays

 Hint   Identify details in the passage. Reread Paragraph 3. Why can starfish live in many different places?

2 The sunflower starfish is different from other starfish because it—

Ⓕ is very soft

Ⓖ has an extra arm

Ⓗ has large eyes

Ⓙ is very tiny

 Hint   Compare the sunflower starfish to other starfish. Find the place in the passage where the sunflower starfish is mentioned. What makes it different from other starfish?

3 Which of these is an *opinion* in the passage?

Ⓐ A starfish does not have a brain.

Ⓑ Most starfish live in shallow water.

Ⓒ A starfish moves with its mouth facing downward.

Ⓓ Starfish are amazing animals.

Hint Remember that an opinion is something that someone believes to be true. It is not a fact. Which of the choices sounds like a belief rather than a fact?

4 What does the word *ability* mean?

Ⓕ Hard shell

Ⓖ Young starfish

Ⓗ Special trait

Ⓙ Difficult job

Hint Here is a vocabulary question. Look at Paragraph 4 again and find the word *ability*. Can you find clues to the meaning of the word? Read the paragraph again. What is the author describing as an ability?

5 How does a starfish use the feet on the bottom of its rays?

_____

_____

_____

_____

_____

_____

 Hint Summarize information from the passage. Look again at Paragraph 4. Read about the starfish's feet. How do these feet help the starfish?

6 Name three ways that a starfish is different from other animals. Explain.

_____

_____

_____

_____

_____

_____

 Hint Compare the starfish to other animals. Look for differences in the passage. Include only those details that clearly show how the starfish is different from most other animals.

Essay question: What makes a starfish an interesting animal? Use details from the passage, along with your own ideas to answer the question.

 You will use a **Main Idea Map** to answer this essay question. Look at the map below.

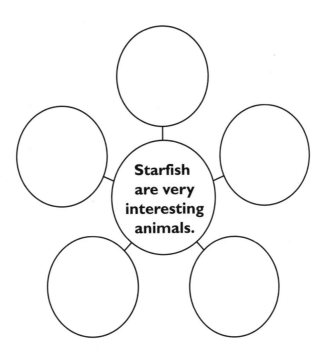

Starfish
are very
interesting
animals.

Remember that a **Main Idea Map** helps you organize your thoughts so that you can answer an essay question based on the main idea of a passage. It has a large bubble in the middle for you to write the main idea in. You can see that the main idea is already filled in on the map above.

It also has smaller bubbles attached to the large bubble. This is where you write details from the passage that help prove your main idea.

Now you will fill in the same **Main Idea Map** on the next page. It will help you answer why starfish are interesting animals.

Fill in the main idea from the passage first. Then search the passage for details that help prove your main idea. Write each detail in a separate smaller bubble. Find as many details in the passage as you can, in order to prove your main idea.

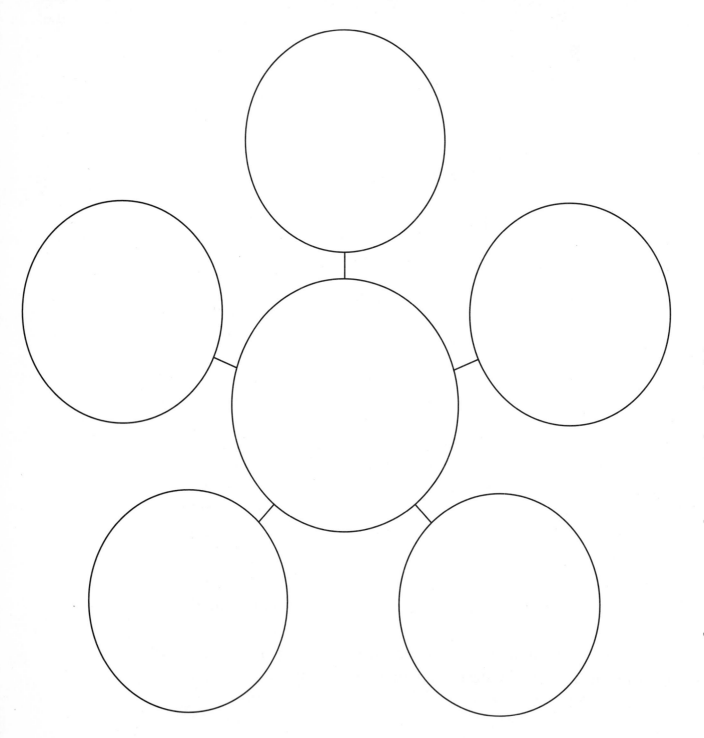

Now that you have filled in the **Main Idea Map,** use it to answer the essay question below. If you need more space, continue writing on a separate sheet of paper.

7 What makes a starfish an interesting animal? Use details from the passage, along with your own ideas to answer the question.

_____

_____

_____

_____

_____

_____

_____

_____

_____

_____

_____

Hint Draw a conclusion based on details from the passage. Look at the information you wrote in the **Main Idea Map.** Start your essay by stating your main idea. Then give the details from the map that help support your main idea.

DIRECTIONS: Read this story about a girl with a special goal. Then answer questions 8 through 16. Darken the circle next to the correct answer choice or write your answer on the lines.

Suprita's New Year

Suprita sat on a chair in the principal's office. She nervously chewed on her fingernails as she waited for Mrs. Henson to finish her telephone conversation.

Mrs. Henson put down the phone and smiled at Suprita. "Hi Suprita," she said. "How are your violin lessons going?"

"Very well, thank you," Suprita replied. "I practice every day for two hours. That is my favorite time of day."

"Would you like to go to a school where music is an important part of every day?" Mrs. Henson asked.

Suprita sat up straight. Her eyes sparkled. "Oh, yes! But—I would have to leave this school." That was a sad idea. Suprita had spent three very happy years in this public school. It was only September, and she was glad to be back with her classmates. She was happy to be in the third grade.

"I'll give you some information about the music school to give to your parents," said Mrs. Henson. "Then you can decide together whether it is better to stay here or try out for the new school."

That evening during dinner, Suprita showed her mother and father the booklet Mrs. Henson had given her. It described a private school where all the students played a musical instrument. Music was a big part of each day.

Suprita's mother looked worried. "Why should she go to a different school?" she asked Suprita's father. "She does very well in her own school.

No, I don't think this is a good idea." She **crumbled** a piece of flat bread called "naan." Suprita's little brother and sister giggled. Suprita knew her mother wanted her to be happy. She knew her mother was worried that Suprita would miss her friends and her old school.

"Maybe we should find out more," Suprita's father said. "Then we can decide."

But Suprita knew she wanted to go to this new school. She wanted to play her violin in school. She wanted to learn more about music. After dinner, Suprita went to her bedroom and read the booklet about the school. Then she quietly asked her father to help her fill out the forms.

In October, the family had planned a visit to Bombay, India, where Suprita's grandparents and cousins lived. There was just one problem. The music school held **auditions** during that week in October. Suprita did not want to miss her chance. If she went to the audition and played her violin well, she might be accepted into the special school.

"Please, Mother, Daddy," she *pleaded*. "Let me stay with Auntie Jaya while everyone else goes to India for the holiday? I just have to get to that audition!"

"I don't know," said her mother. "Don't you want to come with us? It's Dewali, and everyone is expecting us. You should not miss a trip to your home country during the New Year's celebration." Suprita's mother loved her daughter, but she still did not understand how much Suprita wanted to go to this new school.

Dewali was a wonderful Indian holiday. It marked the old Indian New Year. Children had no school for the whole month. Instead, they watched fireworks, visited friends and family, and got lots of presents. If she did not go to Bombay, Suprita would miss out on all of that.

But Suprita really wanted to go to this music school. In the end, she

crumbled = broke into small parts
audition = tryouts, where the best students are chosen

convinced her mother. Her mother helped her pack her suitcase, and she went to stay with Auntie Jaya. While her family was on a plane high over the ocean, Suprita was in Auntie Jaya's living room practicing her violin. Auntie Jaya also worried about Suprita's happiness. But she believed that Suprita could make her own decision about her future and hoped that Suprita would be accepted into the school.

When the big day came, Suprita wore a fresh white blouse and her prettiest skirt. She **clutched** her aunt's hand as she climbed the steep steps to the school's front door. Inside the lobby, Suprita held her breath. There were so many other children there, all with their instruments. She glanced around the lobby. The walls were decorated with musical notes and scrolls of sheet music under glass. Could she really be a student in this place?

When her turn came, Suprita followed a tall, red-haired woman into a small room. Auntie Jaya had to wait in the lobby. Suprita waved, and her aunt gave her a proud smile.

Suprita sat down on the hard chair and opened her violin case. Three people sat facing her. They were the judges. They were the ones who had the power to welcome her or to send her away. Suprita told herself to just think about the music. Then she raised her bow and began to play. She kept her eyes on the instrument and did not look up even once at the judges. That made her feel better. She knew this piece of music. It was like an old friend.

At the end of the piece, Suprita looked up at the judges. They were smiling at her.

"Welcome, Suprita! Next fall, you will be a student at this school," one of them said.

Suprita thanked them and gathered her things. She ran out to her aunt.

"I did it!" Suprita shouted.

"Happy New Year!" said Auntie Jaya. "This is the best present you could get."

> **convinced** = talked into, made her believe
> **clutched** = held closely

8 Which word *best* describes Suprita?

Ⓐ friendly

Ⓑ angry

Ⓒ brave

Ⓓ shy

Hint Interpret a character trait. This information about Suprita is not stated directly in the story, but you can figure out the answer from certain details. Think about the things Suprita does in the story. Which word best describes her actions?

9 Where does the beginning of the story take place?

Ⓕ In Mrs. Henson's office

Ⓖ In the new school

Ⓗ At Suprita's house

Ⓙ At Auntie Jaya's house

Hint This question asks you about the setting at the beginning of the story. The setting shows when and where the story takes place. Go back to the beginning of the story. Where is Suprita?

10 You can tell that the word *pleaded* means—

  Ⓐ shouted

  Ⓑ asked

  Ⓒ begged

  Ⓓ cried

Hint Here is another vocabulary question. You can figure out the meaning of the word from the way Suprita feels about going to the music school. Which word would best describe the way she asks her parents to let her stay at Auntie Jaya's?

11 At first, Suprita's mother does not want Suprita to go to the music school because—

  Ⓕ she thinks she will be unhappy

  Ⓖ she thinks it is too far away

  Ⓗ she thinks she is too young

  Ⓙ she thinks music is silly

Hint Draw a conclusion. Reread the part of the story where Suprita shows her parents the booklet about the music school. Look for clues as to how Suprita's mother feels. Why does she want Suprita to stay at her old school?

12 The boxes show some things that happened in the story.

Suprita shows her parents the booklet about the music school.		Suprita plays her violin in front of the judges.
1	**2**	**3**

What belongs in Box 2?

Ⓐ Mrs. Henson explains about the music school.

Ⓑ Suprita waits for Mrs. Henson to hang up the phone.

Ⓒ The judges tell Suprita she can go to the music school.

Ⓓ Suprita and her aunt wait in the lobby.

 Hint Put the events in order. Find each event in the story. In what order did the events happen? Find the event that comes after Box 1 but before Box 3.

13 What probably happens next in the story?

Ⓕ Suprita flies to India to be with her family.

Ⓖ Suprita calls her parents to share her good news.

Ⓗ Suprita decides to go back to her old school.

Ⓙ Suprita asks the judges for a second chance.

 Hint Extend the story and predict what will happen next. Think about the events in the story. Look at the answer choices. Which ones probably would not happen? Which choice is most likely to happen?

14 What can you tell about Suprita's father from the story? Describe what he is like.

_____

_____

_____

_____

 Hint Determine a character trait. What do you know about Suprita's father? Go back to the part of the story where Suprita shows her family the booklet about the music school. How does Suprita's father act? What do his actions tell about him?

15 Why is Suprita's family going to India?

_____

_____

_____

_____

 Hint Identify details from the story. Find the part of the story that tells why Suprita's family is going to India. What is special about this trip?

Essay question: How is Suprita's mother different from her Auntie Jaya? How are the two alike? Compare and contrast the two characters.

 You will use a **Venn Diagram** to answer this essay question. Look at the map below.

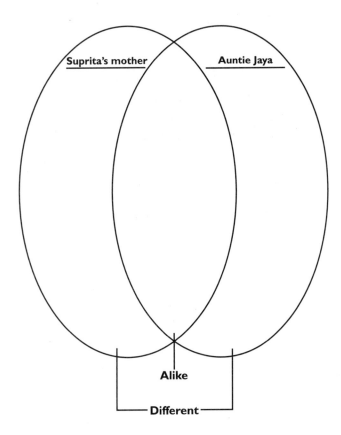

Suprita's mother

Auntie Jaya

Alike

Different

Remember that a **Venn Diagram** helps you compare and contrast two things. There are two large ovals. The name of each of the things being compared and contrasted goes at the top of each oval. You can see that each oval is already labeled on the diagram above.

The ways that the two things are different go in the *outside parts* of the ovals. The ways that the two things are the same go in the *middle part*.

Now you will fill in the same **Venn Diagram** on the next page. It will help you describe how Suprita's mother and Auntie Jaya are different and how they are alike.

Label what you are comparing and contrasting at the top of each oval. Then search the story for details that are different about each character. Write these details in the outside parts of each oval. Then search the story for details that are the same about each character. Write these details in the middle overlapping part of the ovals.

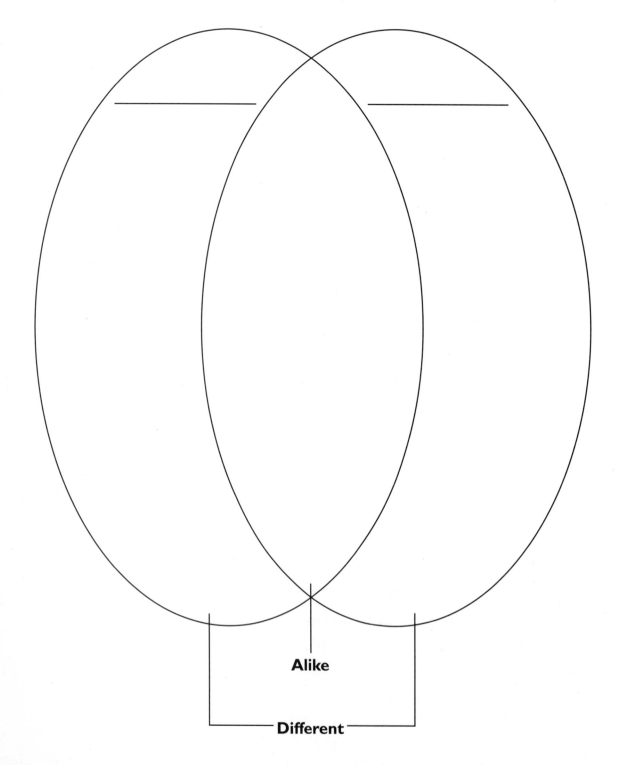

Alike

Different

Now that you have filled in the **Venn Diagram,** use it to answer the essay question below. If you need more space, continue writing on a separate sheet of paper.

16 How is Suprita's mother different from her Auntie Jaya? How are the two alike? Compare and contrast the two characters.

_____

_____

_____

_____

_____

_____

_____

_____

_____

_____

_____

Hint Look at the information you wrote in the **Venn Diagram.** First write how Suprita's mother is different from her Auntie Jaya. Then write how they are alike. Include all of the details that you listed in the diagram to help you answer the essay question.

DIRECTIONS: Read this passage that explains how to make a family tree. Then answer questions 17 through 23. Darken the circle next to the correct answer choice or write your answer on the lines.

Trace Your Family Tree

Do you ever wonder about the people who started your family? You may know some of these people. You may know your grandparents. If you are lucky, you may know your great-grandparents, too. But what about your great-great grandparents? Who were they? What were their names and where did they live?

Creating a family tree is a great way to trace your family's history. A family tree looks a little like a real tree. It has roots, a trunk, and branches. The roots are the people who started the family. The names of all of the people who are part of the family are on the branches.

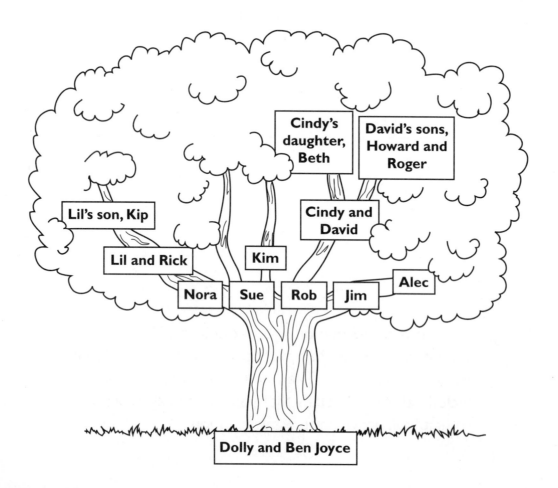

This page may not be reproduced without permission of Steck-Vaughn/Berrent.

Look at the family tree on page 68. Dolly and Ben Joyce are the "roots" of the family tree. Can you find Dolly and Ben's children? Can you find their grandchildren?

To get started, write down your name and the names of your brothers and sisters. Write down your parent's names. Find out the full names of your grandparents and your grandparents' parents. Write down the names of aunts, uncles, and cousins. Ask your parents and grandparents to help you find out the "roots" of your family. (Remember that the "roots" are the people who started your family.) Then, draw a large tree. Put the names of your family on your tree.

You might want to write a story about your family, too. Ask your family members some questions. Use a tape recorder to record their answers. Find some photographs of your family.

Here are some questions to ask your family.

What is your full name?

Where and when were you born?

How many brothers and sisters do you have? What are their names?

Where and when were your parents born? What did they look like? What kinds of jobs did they do?

Did you know your grandparents? Did you ever get to know your great-grandparents? Were these people born in this country or in another country?

Where and when did you get married?

What are the names of your children?

What special stories do your family members share?

You can probably think of other good questions too. When you finish, put your family tree and your story in a safe place. One day, you may be able to show your family tree and read your story to your own children.

17 When you make a family tree, what should you do *first*?

Ⓐ Ask your family some questions.

Ⓑ Write down your name.

Ⓒ Find out the "roots" of your family.

Ⓓ Draw a large tree.

 Hint Identify the order of events. Scan the passage to find out what you should do first when you make a family tree. What does it say after the words "To get started"?

18 Who are Dolly and Ben Joyce's children?

Ⓕ Nora, Sue, Jim, and Rob

Ⓖ Lil and Rick

Ⓗ Liza and Will

Ⓙ Kim, Alec, Cindy, and David

 Hint Interpret information given. Look at the family tree on the page. Which names appear directly above Dolly and Ben Joyce's names?

19 All of these could be part of your family tree *except*—

   Ⓐ the names of your aunts and uncles

   Ⓑ the year your best friend was born

   Ⓒ the birth dates of your cousins

   Ⓓ the name of your great-grandfather

 Hint Here you must decide what does not belong. Remember that a family tree is about your family. Who should be included? Who does not belong on your family tree?

20 What is this passage *mostly* about?

   Ⓕ Asking your family questions

   Ⓖ Making your family tree

   Ⓗ Writing a story about your family

   Ⓙ Finding pictures of your family

 Hint This question asks you to determine the main idea of the passage. Think about what you've learned from the passage. What does it ask you to do?

21 What is a family tree?

_____

_____

_____

_____

_____

 Hint   Summarize information from the passage. Look back at the beginning of the passage. What does it ask you to do?

22 What are the parts of a family tree? Who are the "roots" of the tree?

_____

_____

_____

_____

 Hint   Identify details from the selection. Reread the second paragraph of the passage. The answer is right there. What are the parts of a family tree? Look for a description about the "roots" of the tree.

Essay question: Explain how to make a family tree. Write the steps in order. Use the details in the article to help you with your writing.

 You will use a **Sequence Map** to answer this essay question. Look at the map below.

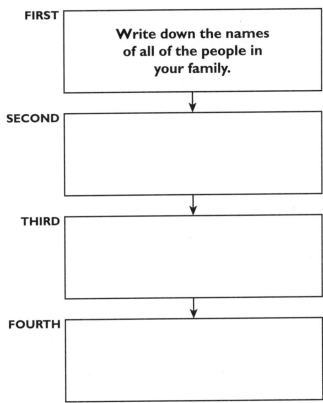

FIRST
> **Write down the names of all of the people in your family.**

SECOND

THIRD

FOURTH

Remember that a **Sequence Map** helps you write a summary of an article, which includes the key points. You will be writing a summary of instructions for making a family tree. The first instruction goes in the top box. You can see that the top box is already filled in on the map above.

The rest of the boxes show what happens second, third, fourth, and so on. This is where you write the rest of the instructions for making a family tree.

Now you will fill in the same **Sequence Map** on the next page. It will help you explain how to make a family tree.

 Find the first step and write it in the top box. Then read the passage until you reach the second step. Fill it in the second box. Continue writing each instruction in the next box down until you reach the end of the passage.

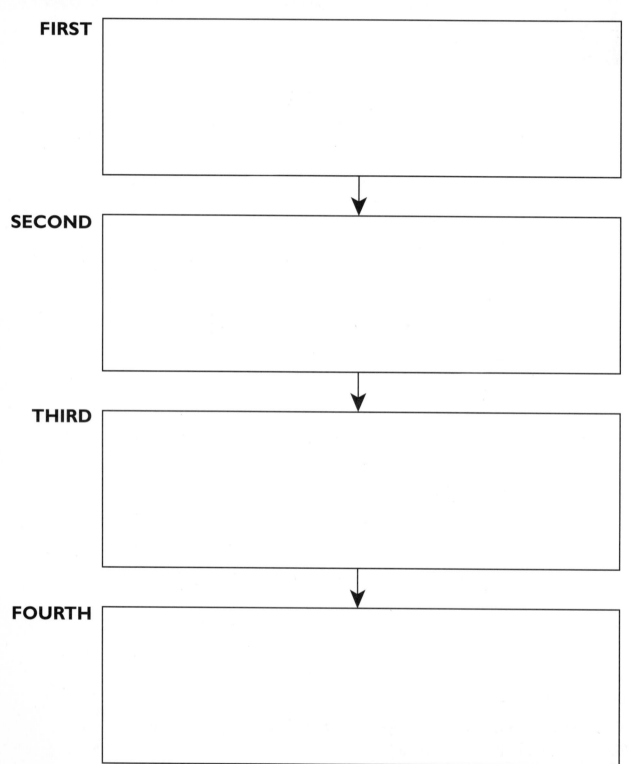

FIRST

SECOND

THIRD

FOURTH

Now that you have filled in the **Sequence Map,** use it to answer the essay question below. If you need more space, continue writing on a separate sheet of paper.

23 Explain how to make a family tree. Write the steps in order. Use the details in the article to help you with your writing.

_____

_____

_____

_____

_____

_____

_____

_____

_____

 Hint Summarize information by putting steps in order. Use the information on the **Sequence Map** to write your essay. Start by stating each important step. Then follow with the details about each step.

 *Speak Out*

You have read about making a family tree. Think about something special that has happened in your own family. Prepare a short speech about this event. Then give your speech to the class.

DIRECTIONS: Read this poem about a child's delight in the night sky. Then answer questions 24 through 30. Darken the circle next to the correct answer choice or write your answer on the lines.

Escape at Bedtime

from *A Child's Garden of Verses*

by Robert Louis Stevenson

The lights from the parlor and kitchen shone out
    Through the blinds and the windows and bars;
And high overhead and all moving about,
    There were thousands of millions of stars.
There ne'er were such thousands of leaves on a tree,
    Nor of people in church or the Park,
As the crowds of the stars that looked down upon me,
    And that *glittered* and winked in the dark.

The Dog, and the Plough, and the Hunter, and all,

And the star of the sailor, and Mars,

These shown in the sky, and the pail by the wall

Would be half full of water and stars.

They saw me at last, and they chased me with cries,

And they soon had me packed into bed;

But the glory kept shining and bright in my eyes,

And the stars going round in my head.

The Dog, and the Plough, and the Hunter = well-known group of stars that form shapes

24 Who is the speaker in this poem?

Ⓐ A mother or father

Ⓑ A child

Ⓒ A star

Ⓓ The sky

 Hint Draw a conclusion about the poem. The speaker is the person who is "telling" what happens. Who is telling the story in this poem? Read the title of the poem for a clue.

25 In the poem, the word *glittered* means—

Ⓕ listened

Ⓖ burned

Ⓗ sparkled

Ⓙ waved

 Hint This is a vocabulary question. If you do not know the meaning of *glittered*, find the word in the poem. Then look at the lines before it. What is the narrator talking about? Which answer choice best tells how a star looks at night?

26 Which word best describes the mood or tone of this poem?

  Ⓐ funny

  Ⓑ frightening

  Ⓒ peaceful

  Ⓓ exciting

 Hint The mood or tone of a poem is the feeling it gives the reader. How does the speaker feel about stars? How does the poem make you feel?

27 What is the setting of the poem?

  Ⓕ The speaker's home

  Ⓖ The speaker's boat

  Ⓗ A park

  Ⓙ A church

 Hint Remember that the setting of a poem is where it takes place. Where is the speaker when he sees the stars?

28 What two things does the speaker compare the stars to? Explain your answer.

_____

_____

_____

_____

_____

_____

 Hint Identify details from the poem. You can find the answer on the first page of the poem.

29 What happens after the speaker is in bed?

_____

_____

_____

_____

_____

_____

Hint Interpret what words from the poem mean. Read the end of the poem after the words "And they soon had packed me into bed." What happens after this?

Essay question: Explain how the speaker of the poem feels at bedtime when he looks up at the sky. Use details from the poem.

You will use a **Setting Map** to answer this essay question. Look at the map below.

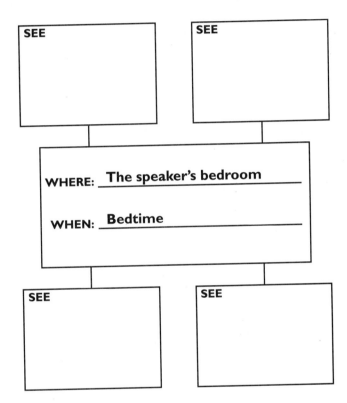

SEE

SEE

WHERE: The speaker's bedroom

WHEN: Bedtime

SEE

SEE

Remember that a **Setting Map** helps you organize the details of what you see, hear, smell, touch, and taste in the poem in order to describe the setting of the poem. It has a box in the middle where you write where and when the poem takes place. You can see that this box is already filled in on the **Setting Map** above.

All of the boxes in this **Setting Map** are labeled "SEE." That is because all of the details the speaker uses are about what he sees. You can fill in the boxes with details from the poem.

Now you will fill in the same **Setting Map** on the next page. It will help you explain how the speaker of the poem feels when he looks at the night sky.

 Write where and when the poem takes place in the middle box. Then fill in the other boxes. All of the boxes are labeled "SEE." That is because the poem is made up of things that the speaker sees. Fill in each of the boxes with a different thing that the speaker sees.

SEE

SEE

WHERE: _____

WHEN: _____

SEE

SEE

Now that you have filled in the **Setting Map,** use it to answer the essay question below. If you need more space, continue writing on a separate sheet of paper.

30 Explain how the speaker of the poem feels at bedtime when he looks up at the sky. Use details from the poem.

_____

_____

_____

_____

_____

_____

_____

_____

_____

_____

_____

Hint

Summarize the poem by describing the setting. Look at the information you wrote in the **Setting Map.** Think about the things that the speaker sees. How do you think they make him feel? Use the details from the map to help explain why you think the speaker feels this way.

Summary

In Unit 3, you read several different passages. Then you answered questions about these passages. For some of these questions, you had to choose the correct answer. These questions are called multiple-choice questions. In this unit, you had hints to help you answer multiple-choice questions.

For other questions in Unit 3, you had to write your own answers. These questions are called open-ended questions. You had hints to help you answer these questions too. Some open-ended questions required a short response of only a few sentences. Other open-ended questions were essay questions that required more writing. You used graphic organizers to plan your response to the essay questions.

You answered literal, interpretive, and critical questions in this unit. Remember that with literal questions you look for meaning. You can find the answer to literal questions right in the passage. With interpretive questions, you have to determine the meaning. You can usually find clues in the passage to help you answer interpretive questions. With critical questions, you go beyond the passage. You make a conclusion about what you've read. You can usually add your own thoughts when you answer a critical question.

Whatever type of selection you read or question you answer, you should always follow the **Four *R*s:**

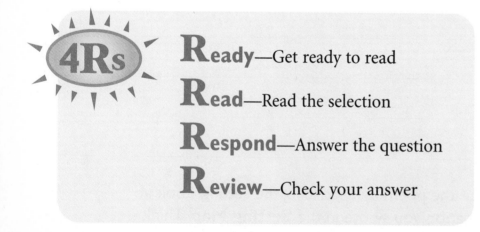

4Rs

Ready—Get ready to read

Read—Read the selection

Respond—Answer the question

Review—Check your answer

UNIT 4

Test

Now you will take a practice test. The test includes all the skills you have reviewed in this book. Follow the directions in each section. As always, remember to use the **Four *R*s: R**eady, **R**ead, **R**espond, and **R**eview. You may look back at the reading passages as needed.

For the multiple-choice questions, work carefully and try to get as many questions right as you can. Do not spend too much time on any one question. If you are not sure of an answer, make the best choice you can and go on to the next question. You can go back and check answers later if you have time.

For the open-ended questions, plan out what you want to say before writing. Use graphic organizers to help you write your essay questions. Make sure that you respond to all parts of each item. After you finish writing, use the checklist on page 30 to help you review your work.

DIRECTIONS: Read this story about two frogs. Then answer questions 1 through 9. Darken the circle next to the correct answer choice or on the separate answer sheet. Write your open-ended answers on the lines.

The Two Frogs: A Japanese Folktale

a retelling

Once upon a time, in Japan, there were two frogs. One frog was big and brown. He lived in Kyoto. The other frog was little and green. He lived in Osaka. Neither frog had ever traveled far from his own home. Strangely enough, one day each had the same idea. The frog from Kyoto would visit Osaka. The frog from Osaka would visit Kyoto.

So on a beautiful spring morning, both frogs found themselves hopping along the road from Kyoto to Osaka. Of course, they were each coming from a different direction. The trip took longer than they had expected. In fact, the frogs soon became quite tired. These frogs did not know much about the land and were surprised to come upon a great mountain halfway between Kyoto and Osaka. Climbing the mountain was very hard work for such little animals. Huffing and puffing, they struggled up the mountain. What a surprise! At the mountain top, the two frogs came face to face.

They stared at each other *speechlessly*. Then the frog from Kyoto said, "What brings you here, brother?"

"I am bound for the great city of Kyoto," explained the frog from Osaka. "I would like to gaze on the Mikado's **wondrous** palace."

"My, how interesting!" exclaimed the frog from Kyoto. "That is where I come from. I'm just on my way to visit Osaka, a town I have never seen."

wondrous = wonderful

"And Osaka is where I live!" replied the other frog. "This is truly a **coincidence**."

It was growing warm, and the two tired creatures lay down to rest a while in a bed of cool leaves. Each was thinking that the journey was much too long, when suddenly the Osaka frog said, "Too bad we are not taller. Then we could see both towns from this mountain top and decide whether we should take the trouble to finish our journeys."

"Well, I have an idea," the Kyoto frog answered. "Let's just stand up on our hind legs and hold onto one another. Then each of us can look at the town he is headed for."

This idea seemed good to his **companion.** So the two frogs stood up on their hind legs, holding onto each other so that they would not fall down. The frogs had a very good view of the countryside. But they made a very foolish mistake. You see, a frog's eyes lie toward the back of its head. The frog sees what is behind it, not what is in front of it! What do you think happened?

That's right. The Osaka frog saw Osaka, the place he had just come from. And the Kyoto frog saw Kyoto, the place where he was born.

"For goodness sake!" cried the Osaka frog. "Kyoto looks just like Osaka! It is a waste of time to go any further."

The Kyoto frog agreed with him. "It's quite true. The two towns are exactly alike. Now we can each go home and know that we have not missed a thing."

So the frogs shook hands and wished one another well. Then each hopped on home.

And for the rest of their lives, these two silly animals believed that Kyoto and Osaka were just alike.

coincidence = events that happen at the same time by accident
companion = friend

1 The boxes show some things that happened in the story.

The frogs reach the top of the mountain.		The frogs each decide to return home.
1	2	3

What belongs in Box 2?

Ⓐ The frogs each plan to make a journey.

Ⓑ The frogs decide that their home towns look alike.

Ⓒ The frogs wish to see new places.

Ⓓ The frogs are glad to be back home again.

2 You can tell that the word *speechlessly* means—

Ⓕ with anger

Ⓖ without excitement

Ⓗ with joy

Ⓙ without talking

3 What does each frog actually see when he stands up on his hind legs?

Ⓐ The town he lives in

Ⓑ The clouds in the sky

Ⓒ The mountains he stands on

Ⓓ The place he is going to

4 Which is an *opinion* from the story?

   Ⓕ Frogs see what is behind them.

   Ⓖ Frogs are foolish creatures.

   Ⓗ The frogs met on top of a mountain.

   Ⓙ The frogs were traveling to different places.

5 You can tell from the story that in the future the frogs will probably—

   Ⓐ travel to a new town

   Ⓑ stay at home

   Ⓒ write letters to each other

   Ⓓ climb the mountain again

6 What lesson do we learn from this story?

   Ⓕ Friends have a lot in common.

   Ⓖ Frogs are better off at home.

   Ⓗ All places look the same.

   Ⓙ Think about what you see.

7 Why did the frogs think the cities they were traveling to looked just like their hometowns?

_____

_____

_____

_____

_____

_____

8 What does the author think about the two frogs? Use examples from the story to support your answer.

_____

_____

_____

_____

_____

_____

Essay question: Describe the two frogs. Explain how the frogs are alike and how they are different.

Look at the **Venn Diagram** below.

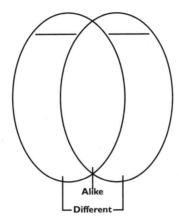

Alike

Different

You will draw your own **Venn Diagram** on the next page. Label your diagram and fill in the ovals with what is alike and what is different about the two frogs.

Draw a **Venn Diagram** below to help you compare and contrast the two frogs in the story. Once you have drawn your diagram and filled it in, use it to answer the essay question on the next page.

9 Describe the two frogs. Explain how the frogs are alike and how they are different.

If you need more space, continue writing on a separate sheet of paper.

_____

_____

_____

_____

_____

_____

_____

_____

_____

_____

_____

_____

_____

DIRECTIONS: **Read this poem about some toys that talk about their experiences in the world. Then answer questions 10 through 18. Darken the circle next to the correct answer choice or on the separate answer sheet. Write your open-ended answers on the lines.**

The Toys Talk of the World

by Katharine Pyle

'I should like,' said the vase from the china-store,
'To have seen the world a little more.

'When they carried me here I was wrapped up tight,
But they say it is really a lovely sight.'

'Yes,' said a little plaster bird,
'That is exactly what *I* have heard;

'There are thousands of trees, and oh, what a sight
It must be when the candles are all alight.'

The fat top rolled on his other side:
'It is not in the least like that,' he cried.

'Except myself and the kite and ball,
None of you know of the world at all.

'There are houses, and pavements hard and red,
And everything spins around,' he said;

'Sometimes it goes slowly, and sometimes fast,
And it often stops with a bump at last.'

The wooden donkey nodded his head:
'I had heard the world was like that,' he said.

The kite and ball *exchanged* a smile,
But they did not speak; it was not worth while.

10 Where does this poem probably take place?

ⓐ A store

ⓑ A backyard

ⓒ A garden

ⓓ A barn

11 From this poem you can conclude that the vase has not seen the world because it—

ⓕ has been broken

ⓖ was in a box

ⓗ was rolled around

ⓙ does not have eyes

12 Why does the top think everything in the world is spinning?

ⓐ He was traveling in a car when he saw it.

ⓑ He was turning fast when he saw it.

ⓒ He saw the world through a window.

ⓓ He heard this from the kite and the ball.

13 Another word for *exchanged* is—

   Ⓕ covered

   Ⓖ changed

   Ⓗ traded

   Ⓙ noticed

14 The poem is *mostly* about—

   Ⓐ why people keep old toys

   Ⓑ what the world is like

   Ⓒ why toys want to be outside

   Ⓓ what it is like to be free

15 The kite and the ball have seen the world because they—

   Ⓕ are very old

   Ⓖ are outdoor toys

   Ⓗ were special gifts

   Ⓙ used to live outdoors

16 Read these lines from the poem.

> **The kite and ball exchanged a smile,**
>
> **But they did not speak; it was not worth while.**

Why do the kite and the ball think it is not worthwhile to speak?

_____

_____

_____

_____

_____

17 Why does the top believe that only he, the kite, and the ball know about the world?

_____

_____

_____

_____

_____

Essay question: We all see the world around us in different ways. You have just read a poem that includes several voices. Describe the different views of the world expressed in this poem.

Look at the **Main Idea Map** below.

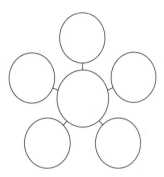

You will draw your own **Main Idea Map** on the next page. Label your map and fill in the bubbles with the main idea and details from the poem that help prove your main idea.

Draw a **Main Idea Map** below to help you describe the different views of the world expressed in this poem. Once you have drawn your map and filled it in, use it to answer the essay question on the next page.

18 We all see the world around us in different ways. You have just read a poem that includes several voices. Describe the different views of the world expressed in this poem.

If you need more space, continue writing on a separate sheet of paper.

_____

_____

_____

_____

_____

_____

_____

_____

_____

_____

_____

_____

_____

DIRECTIONS: Here is a fun gardening project to do with your family and friends. Read the instructions carefully. Then answer questions 19 through 27. Darken the circle next to the correct answer choice or on the separate answer sheet. Write your open-ended answers on the lines.

How to Make a Sunflower Fort

Have you ever built a fort? With a little work, you can grow a fort in your own backyard. Sunflowers are giant yellow flowers. Some sunflowers grow to be over eight feet tall! If you plant sunflower seeds in rows, they will grow into a sunflower fort. A sunflower fort is easy to grow and fun to watch! Follow these steps to grow a beautiful sunflower fort in your backyard.

1. Gather your supplies.

Several packs of sunflower seeds

Rake

String

Watering can

2. Pick a place for your fort.

Before you begin, you need to find a good place for your fort. Ask a grownup to help you find a sunny spot in your yard. Sunflowers are *hardy,* so you can plant them in any type of soil.

3. Map out your fort.

Use string to "map out" your fort. You can grow a small fort or a big fort. Put the string on the ground in the shape of a square or rectangle. Remove grass and rocks from the area. Rake the soil so it's smooth. Mark a spot for your fort's door. You won't plant any seeds in this spot.

4. Plant your seeds.

Lay the seeds out on the ground near the string in rows of two. Not all of the sunflower seeds will grow. And, if they do, your walls will be nice and thick! The seeds should be about two feet apart. Push them about ½-inch into the ground. Don't worry if your seeds are not in perfect rows! Sunflowers grow to be very big. You won't notice if your rows are not perfectly straight.

5. Water and weed the fort.

Give your seeds a little bit of water twice a day until the plants sprout. Then water only once a day. Stake your sunflowers when they are about one-foot high. (When you "stake" a sunflower, you tie it loosely to a stick so that it doesn't fall over. You will need a grownup's help to stake your sunflowers.) Pull out any weeds near your sunflowers as they grow.

6. Enjoy your fort!

Sunflowers grow very quickly. Sometimes, they will grow a whole foot in only one day! Before you know it, you will have a beautiful sunflower fort to show your friends!

19 What should you do *first* when you plant a sunflower fort?

   Ⓐ Pick a place.

   Ⓑ Plant the seeds.

   Ⓒ Map out the fort.

   Ⓓ Gather supplies.

20 You can tell that the word *hardy* means—

   Ⓕ fun to watch

   Ⓖ tall and pretty

   Ⓗ easy to grow

   Ⓙ thin and weak

21 How far apart should you plant sunflower seeds?

   Ⓐ ½ inch

   Ⓑ 6 inches

   Ⓒ 2 feet

   Ⓓ 8 feet

22 You should stake your sunflowers so they do not—

    Ⓕ fall over

    Ⓖ grow too big

    Ⓗ turn around

    Ⓙ break off

23 How often should you water your sunflower seeds before they sprout?

    Ⓐ Once a day

    Ⓑ Every other day

    Ⓒ Twice a day

    Ⓓ Once a week

24 The author probably wrote this passage to—

    Ⓕ tell the reader what sunflowers are like

    Ⓖ teach the reader how to grow a sunflower fort

    Ⓗ show the reader what a sunflower fort is like

    Ⓙ tell the reader a story about a sunflower fort

25 What is a sunflower fort?

_____

_____

_____

_____

_____

_____

_____

26 Describe a good place to grow a sunflower fort.

_____

_____

_____

_____

_____

_____

_____

Essay question: Write a letter to a friend telling him or her how to build a sunflower fort. Use details from the article.

Look at the **Sequence Map** below.

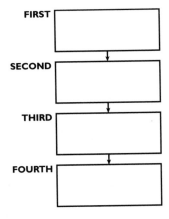

FIRST

SECOND

THIRD

FOURTH

You will draw your own **Sequence Map** on the next page. Fill in the boxes with the steps to building a sunflower fort.

Draw a **Sequence Map** below to help you organize the steps to building a sunflower fort. This will help you write your letter. Once you have drawn your map and filled it in, use it to answer the essay question on the next page.

27 Write a letter to a friend telling him or her how to build a
sunflower fort. Use details from the article.

If you need more space, continue writing on a separate sheet of paper.

_____

_____

_____

_____

_____

_____

_____

_____

_____

_____

_____

Speak Out

Prepare a short speech about something you have made or
built. Give the speech to your classmates. Be prepared to
answer any questions about the steps needed to complete
the project.

DIRECTIONS: **Read this story about Gregory's day in the country. Then answer questions 28 through 39. Darken the circle next to the correct answer choice or on the separate answer sheet. Write your open-ended answers on the lines.**

A Day in the Country

Gregory kicked at the huge piles of leaves on Grandpa's lawn. He had never seen so many dried up leaves in his life. There were some scattered on the sidewalks of Gregory's neighborhood in the city, but never enough to make mountains like these! It was colder here, too. Gregory guessed the city's tall buildings made the air warmer, somehow. But Gregory did not mind the cold. It was fun to spend a weekend with his grandparents. There was always so much to do here in the country.

Smoke drifted up from the chimney of the yellow house where Grandpa and Grandma had lived ever since they were married. The smoke had a woodsy smell. After Gregory and Grandpa finished raking up leaves, they were going to roast chestnuts and make popcorn. That was another thing that was different about country life. You did not buy your hot chestnuts from the vendor in the park. You did not put a bag of popcorn in the microwave oven. Gregory thought it was more exciting the way Grandma prepared these snacks. He and his grandmother agreed that homemade treats were the tastiest.

Gregory made more piles of crisp, golden leaves with his rake. He jumped in them and made crunching sounds. Then he paused to catch his breath. Something funny was going on. Several plump squirrels were racing all over the yard. Each would stop, dig, and run off again. They did not chase each other up the tree today or play any other games. What were the squirrels up to? The one nearest him had fat cheeks. He chattered angrily at another squirrel that came too close. Grandpa looked at the furry animal and laughed. "See that fellow? He's gathering acorns because he knows winter is coming."

"What will he and his squirrel friends do then?" Gregory asked.

"Well, squirrels have ways of getting through the cold months. They store their food to eat later. They keep each other warm by huddling together. And do you see how plump these squirrels look? They've grown thick coats for the new season."

"That's pretty smart of them," Gregory decided.

"Nature is pretty smart," Grandpa replied. He pointed up to the cloudless blue sky. "Do you see those geese?" The birds flew overhead, honking loudly.

"They're flying in a V shape! Do they do that on purpose?" Gregory asked.

"Yes, that is how they travel." Grandpa said. "They go in groups because that makes the trip safer. They are migrating. Do you know what that word means?"

"Yes, our teacher said some birds travel to places where it is warmer. But Grandpa, how do they know just when it's time to go?"

Grandpa leaned on his rake. He smiled at Gregory. "That's a very good question. Scientists figure that the weather and the amount of daylight are clues. In the fall, it gets chillier and the days get shorter. The birds sense this."

"How do they know where they're going?"

"Oh, they follow the sun, the moon, and the stars. I guess there is a compass in those little heads."

"Wow!" Gregory thought for a few moments. "Are they the only animals that migrate?"

"No, some butterflies and moths do. And there are fish that migrate, too."

The screen door slammed. Out came Grandma with mugs of hot chocolate. "Yum, that smells delicious," Gregory shouted. He took a warm cup in his hand.

Grandma smiled. "I figured that since you were taking a break, it was snack time."

"We're not just resting," Grandpa told her. "We're talking about science."

"I'm learning about what animals do in winter," Gregory explained.

"Yes, soon you won't be able to see the little chipmunks. They'll all be hibernating," Grandma said.

"I was just getting to that," Grandpa nodded. "Chipmunks go into a deep sleep in winter. They eat a lot in the autumn. Then, they find a nice cozy spot and curl up. They only wake up when it's time to eat a bit more, and then—back to sleep!"

"Bears do that," Gregory said. He had once read a story about a brown bear that slept through most of the winter in a cave.

"So do skunks and bats," Grandma added. "But not all creatures are so lucky. Not all birds migrate. Deer and rabbits spend the winter months searching for food. They work hard just to stay alive. Sometimes, in the early morning, I see a deer nibbling the tree bark in our yard. We have a red fox, too. He likes to come around here by my berry bushes in the summer. But there are no berries in winter.

"Then what does he eat?" asked Gregory.

"I'm afraid he eats mice," Grandma replied.

"Ugh," her grandson shuddered.

"It's all part of nature's plan," Grandpa shrugged.

Grandma took their empty cups. "Hurry and finish raking, men. I have a pound of chestnuts just waiting for the fire."

"Popcorn too, right, Grandma?

"Certainly," Grandma smiled. "Lucky for us we have a warm house for winter." And she went to get some birdseed to fill up the feeder that perched in the big maple tree.

28 Grandma makes popcorn over the coals in the fireplace because—

Ⓐ she does not have a mirowave oven

Ⓑ that is how Gregory's mother makes popcorn

Ⓒ that is the only way to make popcorn

Ⓓ the popcorn tastes best this way

29 You can tell from the story that the word *shuddered* means—

Ⓕ shook

Ⓖ laughed

Ⓗ grinned

Ⓙ hopped

30 Why will the squirrels huddle together in winter?

Ⓐ To escape the fox

Ⓑ To travel safely

Ⓒ To keep warm

Ⓓ To raise their young

3 1 Which of these is an *opinion* from the story?

    Ⓕ Geese migrate in a V shape.

    Ⓖ Grandma makes the best hot cocoa.

    Ⓗ Skunks hibernate during the cold months.

    Ⓙ Some insects migrate in the winter.

3 2 How does Gregory feel when he learns that the fox eats the mice?

    Ⓐ curious

    Ⓑ upset

    Ⓒ calm

    Ⓓ delighted

3 3 What does Grandma do after she takes the empty cups from Grandpa and Gregory?

    Ⓕ Helps rake the leaves

    Ⓖ Tells Gregory about the deer

    Ⓗ Goes to fill up the birdfeeder

    Ⓙ Washes the cups inside

34 Which word means almost the same as *gathering*?

Ⓐ collecting

Ⓑ hiding

Ⓒ sorting

Ⓓ cracking

35 Geese know it is time to travel because—

Ⓕ other birds fly away south

Ⓖ they have a compass to guide them

Ⓗ their animal friends grow thicker coats

Ⓙ the days become shorter and colder

36 How does Grandpa feel when Gregory asks him questions about animal habits?

Ⓐ angry

Ⓑ unsure

Ⓒ proud

Ⓓ pleased

37 Why does Gregory think the squirrels are acting differently today?

_____

_____

_____

_____

_____

_____

38 How did Grandma say "soon you won't be able to see the little chipmunks"?

_____

_____

_____

_____

_____

_____

Essay Question: What is it like for Gregory to spend a day outdoors in the country? Use details from the story.

Look at the **Setting Map** below.

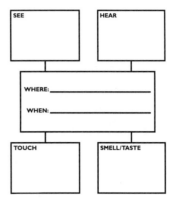

You will draw your own **Setting Map** on the next page. Write where and when Gregory spends a day learning about animals. Then fill in the boxes with what Gregory sees, hears, touches, smells, and tastes.

Draw a **Setting Map** below to help you describe what it is like for Gregory to spend a day outdoors in the country. Once you have drawn your map and filled it in, use it to answer the essay question on the next page.

39 What is it like for Gregory to spend a day outdoors in the country?
Use details from the story.

If you need more space, continue writing on a separate sheet of paper.

_____

_____

_____

_____

_____

_____

_____

_____

_____

_____

_____

_____

_____

_____

DIRECTIONS: Read this advertisement for a new amusement park. Then answer questions 40 through 48. Darken the circle next to the correct answer choice or on the separate answer sheet. Write your open-ended answers on the lines.

SUNNY DAZÉ

FUN PARK

Attention parents and kids of all ages!

Park gates open at 10:00 A.M. on May 21! The Fun Park is open from 10:00 A.M. to 10:00 P.M. every day of the week for the whole summer!

Here are just a few of our exciting rides and amusements:

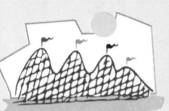

The Twist-and-Shout Roller Coaster—Swoop and soar on our brand new, thrill-packed roller coaster! Parents will be glad to know it's safe for both children and adults.

The Big Splash Water Slide—Slide into our sparkling pool. Children must be eight years or older to purchase tickets for the water slide. Life vests must be worn at all times.

Spooky Secrets Haunted House—A tour through our Spooky Secrets Haunted House will make you shiver. Children under 12 must have an adult with them.

Proud Ponies Carousel—The perfect ride for the younger children in your family. Adults can relax in a carriage built for four. The Proud Ponies Carousel is good, old-fashioned fun.

40 Sunny Daze Fun Park will open on—

    Ⓕ   May 2

    Ⓖ   May 21

    Ⓗ   June 6

    Ⓙ   June 12

41 What ride is best for young children?

    Ⓐ   The Twist-and-Shout Roller Coaster

    Ⓑ   Proud Ponies Carousel

    Ⓒ   Spooky Secrets Haunted House

    Ⓓ   The Big Splash Water Slide

42 An eight-year-old who wants to go into the Spooky Secrets Haunted House must—

    Ⓕ   wear a life vest

    Ⓖ   buy a special ticket

    Ⓗ   go with an adult

    Ⓙ   wear a seatbelt

43 At the end of the Big Splash Water Slide is a—

Ⓐ house

Ⓑ town

Ⓒ pillow

Ⓓ pool

44 Which of these is a *fact* in the passage?

Ⓕ The roller coaster is the best ride in the park.

Ⓖ The Spooky Secrets Haunted House will make you shiver.

Ⓗ The park will be open every day for the whole summer.

Ⓙ The Proud Ponies Carousel is a lot of fun.

45 You can tell from the passage that—

Ⓐ some parents worry that roller coasters are not safe

Ⓑ water slides may not be safe for children

Ⓒ most children at the park ride the roller coaster

Ⓓ kids do not like to ride the Proud Ponies Carousel

46 Why is the Proud Ponies Carousel fun for both parents and children?

_____

_____

_____

_____

_____

_____

_____

47 What should children know before going to the park to ride the Big Splash Water Slide?

_____

_____

_____

_____

_____

_____

_____

Essay Question: What is it like at Sunny Daze Fun Park? Using details from the advertisement, tell about the park and what it is like to visit it.

Look at the **Main Idea Map** below.

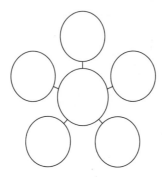

You will draw your own **Main Idea Map** on the next page. Label your map and fill in the bubbles with the main idea and details from the advertisement that help prove your main idea.

Draw a **Main Idea Map** below to help you tell what it is like at Sunny Daze Fun Park. Once you have drawn your map and filled it in, use it to answer the essay question on the next page.

48 What is it like at Sunny Daze Fun Park? Using details from the
advertisement, tell about the park and what it is like to visit it.

If you need more space, continue writing on a separate sheet of paper.

_____

_____

_____

_____

_____

_____

_____

_____

_____

_____

_____

_____

_____

Answer Sheet

STUDENT'S NAME		SCHOOL:
LAST	FIRST	MI	TEACHER:

FEMALE ○   MALE ○

Name grid columns: bubbles A–Z for each letter position.

BIRTH DATE

MONTH	DAY	YEAR
Jan ○	⓪ ⓪	⑦ ⓪
Feb ○	① ①	⑧ ①
Mar ○	② ②	⑨ ②
Apr ○	③ ③	⓪ ③
May ○	④	④
Jun ○	⑤	⑤
Jul ○	⑥	⑥
Aug ○	⑦	⑦
Sep ○	⑧	⑧
Oct ○	⑨	⑨
Nov ○		
Dec ○		

GRADE ② ③ ④ ⑤ ⑥

Reading & Writing Excellence Level C

TEST

1 Ⓐ Ⓑ Ⓒ Ⓓ	9 essay	17 short-answer	25 short-answer	33 Ⓕ Ⓖ Ⓗ Ⓙ	41 Ⓐ Ⓑ Ⓒ Ⓓ
2 Ⓕ Ⓖ Ⓗ Ⓙ	10 Ⓐ Ⓑ Ⓒ Ⓓ	18 essay	26 short-answer	34 Ⓐ Ⓑ Ⓒ Ⓓ	42 Ⓕ Ⓖ Ⓗ Ⓙ
3 Ⓐ Ⓑ Ⓒ Ⓓ	11 Ⓕ Ⓖ Ⓗ Ⓙ	19 Ⓐ Ⓑ Ⓒ Ⓓ	27 essay	35 Ⓕ Ⓖ Ⓗ Ⓙ	43 Ⓐ Ⓑ Ⓒ Ⓓ
4 Ⓕ Ⓖ Ⓗ Ⓙ	12 Ⓐ Ⓑ Ⓒ Ⓓ	20 Ⓕ Ⓖ Ⓗ Ⓙ	28 Ⓐ Ⓑ Ⓒ Ⓓ	36 Ⓐ Ⓑ Ⓒ Ⓓ	44 Ⓕ Ⓖ Ⓗ Ⓙ
5 Ⓐ Ⓑ Ⓒ Ⓓ	13 Ⓕ Ⓖ Ⓗ Ⓙ	21 Ⓐ Ⓑ Ⓒ Ⓓ	29 Ⓕ Ⓖ Ⓗ Ⓙ	37 short-answer	45 Ⓐ Ⓑ Ⓒ Ⓓ
6 Ⓕ Ⓖ Ⓗ Ⓙ	14 Ⓐ Ⓑ Ⓒ Ⓓ	22 Ⓕ Ⓖ Ⓗ Ⓙ	30 Ⓐ Ⓑ Ⓒ Ⓓ	38 short-answer	46 short-answer
7 short-answer	15 Ⓕ Ⓖ Ⓗ Ⓙ	23 Ⓐ Ⓑ Ⓒ Ⓓ	31 Ⓕ Ⓖ Ⓗ Ⓙ	39 essay	47 short-answer
8 short-answer	16 short-answer	24 Ⓕ Ⓖ Ⓗ Ⓙ	32 Ⓐ Ⓑ Ⓒ Ⓓ	40 Ⓕ Ⓖ Ⓗ Ⓙ	48 essay